LORD,
I'M TORN
BETWEEN TWO
MASTERS

LORD, I'M TORN BETWEEN TWO MASTERS

KAY ARTHUR

MULTNOMAH BOOKS • SISTERS, OREGON

LORD, I'M TORN BETWEEN TWO MASTERS

published by Multnomah Books
a part of the Questar publishing family

© 1996 by Kay Arthur

International Standard Book Number: 0-88070-886-7

Portions of this study were previously included in the book
Lord, How Can I Ever Be Righteous.

Design by David Uttley
Cover illustration by Allen Garns

Printed in the United States of America

Unless otherwise identified, Scripture quotations are from:

New American Standard Bible (NASB) ©1960, 1977 by the Lockman Foundation

Also quoted:

The King James Version (KJV)

For information:
QUESTAR PUBLISHERS, INC. • POST OFFICE BOX 1720 • SISTERS, OREGON 97759

96 97 98 99 00 01 02 — 10 9 8 7 6 5 4 3 2 1

CONTENTS

MY PLEDGE TO YOU

You may find this hard to believe, but within a few days or weeks you may want to send this attractive new book sailing rapidly across the room in the general direction of a wall. That's the way it is sometimes, when books get under our skin and prod us in ways we don't want to be prodded. We feel like tossing them rather than dealing with the issues they present.

But if you stick with me, my friend, and diligently seek the Lord through this study, I will make a pledge to you.

I believe with all my heart that you will find the grip of this old world of ours — with all its treasures, promises, problems, and pains — begin to lessen its hold on you. As you dig into our Lord's Sermon on the Mount and cry out to His Holy Spirit for illumination, you will find a new freedom to entwine your thoughts, hopes, dreams, and desires around heavenly things. Eternal things.

You will find yourself choosing to serve the King of kings with all your heart, mind, soul, body...and strength. And, oh, how you are needed at His side! Your life will become an encouragement, a provocation, and a living example to others struggling with the grip of this world. In you, they will see what it means to be a true bondservant of our Lord Jesus Christ.

If you've done much hiking, you know that some trails start out level and gradually get steeper. Others start right off with an uphill climb! The first few weeks of this study are like that second trail. The climb is a little steep at times...but wait until you get to that lookout point where you can see the view! You will have the context and perspective for the life-changing chapters which follow. And just as in my earlier book, *Lord, Only You Can Change Me,* life-change is what this book is all about.

As this study progresses, the lessons get gutsy and practical — they hit us where we live! But that's good. Because the more you learn, listen, and obey, the more you will find yourself freed — strand by strand — from that which ties you to this world and keeps you from being holy as He is holy.

How glorious that freedom is! What an inner sense of well-being it produces. And what a confidence will be yours in your relationship with your heavenly Father.

You need not be torn between two masters, Beloved. You can choose that narrow path that climbs toward glory. You can choose to seek His kingdom and His righteousness. Then, when the kingdom of heaven finally comes to earth, you will see that it was worth every sacrifice. No matter what the cost, no matter what the price, it was worth it all!

"Behold, I am coming quickly, and My reward is with Me, to render to every man according to what he has done." (Revelation 22:12)

WHAT IS
THE KINGDOM
OF HEAVEN?

D A Y   O N E

C aron signaled Ted as she pulled out of the drive, happily letting her fingers spell out their silent code of love.

Ted signaled back, "I love you."

Watching until Caron's car was out of sight, Ted shut the front door and smiled. It hadn't been easy, but he and Caron had nothing to be ashamed of in their courtship...nothing to diminish the delight and discovery of their wedding night. From the time they began dating, they had determined to be obedient to God. They had kept themselves pure.

It was Sunday evening, and their pastor's message from Revelation 19 — "The Bride of Christ" — had dominated their discussion as they wrapped gifts for the bridesmaids and groomsmen. Their conversation had been filled with dreams and visions.... How could their marriage reflect their love of the Lord? How could their union demonstrate their commitment to His kingdom, their desire to be clothed in linen, bright and clean — woven by "the righteous acts of the saints"?

It had been such a wonderful evening, warmed with love, shared dreams, and anticipation.

It was also the last evening they would spend together on earth.

Just minutes after leaving her fiancé's house, Caron suddenly found herself face to face with her heavenly Bridegroom. Yards from her own driveway, her car was broadsided by a speeding drunk driver, and she was instantly killed.

Just think of stepping on shore and finding it heaven,
of touching a hand and finding it God's,
of breathing new air and finding it celestial,
of waking up in glory and finding it home![1]

Instead of a wedding, there was a funeral.

It was unexpected by everyone — except a sovereign, loving God. Because of the way they had lived and loved, they could stand before that God without shame...Caron in heaven, Ted on earth. Ted had neither tarnished nor violated the one who had been purchased by the death, burial, and resurrection of their Lord Jesus Christ. As Ted looked down on his beloved in her coffin, dressed in her white bridal gown, he caught the fragrance from the bridal bouquet. If she had lived, Caron would have carried it down the aisle. Now, it adorned her casket.

Through it all, however, Ted never questioned the sovereign God whom He loved and trusted. No, he didn't understand His Lord's reasons for taking Caron home at that particular time, in that particular way. He might never understand those reasons. But he determined to cling in faith's obedience to all he knew about God. The kingdom of heaven was their possession. Caron was home now. Someday he would see her again...face to face.

Have you ever wondered, my friend, what the kingdom of heaven is all about?

When tragedy falls out of a clear blue sky, when life presses in, when circumstances seem confused or painful, have you ever found yourself wondering what this heavenly kingdom is all about? To whom does it belong? When will it arrive? What does it look like? Is it something for the next life only, or can it be experienced today?

If you have pondered these things, you are wise. Death in our world is as certain as life, and just as we prepare ourselves to live, so we must prepare ourselves to die. Scripture says, "it is appointed for men to die once and after this *comes* judgment" (Hebrews 9:27). The one who masters you in life will be your master in death. Therefore as we begin — or perhaps continue — our study of the Sermon on the Mount, let's launch our journey with a look at what we can learn about the kingdom of heaven.

Since the Sermon on the Mount is only three chapters long, take a few minutes to read it through. You will find it printed out on pages 243 to 250. As you read, mark each occurrence of the word *kingdom* or the phrase *kingdom of heaven* in a special color or special way. You might simply want to highlight it in blue and draw a little cloud around it like this: ⌒⌒⌒⌒. If you already did this exercise in our initial study of the Sermon on the Mount, *Lord, Only You Can Change Me*, you will find it profitable to do again. The more you read the Sermon on the Mount, especially aloud, and the more you mark and study the text, the more it will become a part of you. And if it truly becomes a part of you, Beloved, you will not be ashamed when you see your Lord and Savior face to face.

When you finish marking every occurrence of the words *kingdom* or *kingdom of heaven*, list below what you learn about the kingdom of heaven. Note the chapter and verse where you found the reference. Don't add anything to what the text says…the text is all we want at this point.

INSIGHTS ON THE KINGDOM OF HEAVEN
FROM THE SERMON ON THE MOUNT

Now…a little food for thought as we call it a day. According to what you have learned from marking these references to the kingdom of heaven, what would be *your* status if you, like Caron, were suddenly taken in death? Where would you find yourself when your spirit left your body?

If you were to find yourself in heaven, according to Matthew 5:19 would you be called "great" or "least" in the kingdom?

What is the basis of your answer?

Would you like to be among those called "great" — and have a deep assurance in your heart that this will remain your status? If so, my friend, keep studying. These nine weeks will pass quickly, but I don't believe they will go unchallenged in your life. There is an enemy who wants to keep you in darkness, who wants to entice you to sin, who doesn't want you to know the truth. It is *truth* which keeps you from "the lie" and the "father of lies." Don't give in to him, Beloved. Persevere! It is well worth it.

DAY TWO

If you were to analyze the people of your nation as a whole, who — or what — would you say is their master? It is what masters a people — what captures their minds, their wills, and their bodies — that makes them what they are and determines how they live.

Take a good look around you. Think about your friends and associates. Consider the lifestyles of the so-called rich and famous. Watch the down-and-outers, the alcoholics, drug addicts, and amoral. What is the dominating factor of their lives? Where are they headed as a result of what or who has gained mastery over them? It is a wise person who considers these pathways — and their ultimate destinations — before choosing to follow a hero or role model. *Where do these lifestyles lead? What is their end result?* Ultimately it is not what we know that determines our destiny but what we *do*, what we allow to rule our lives.

The Sermon on the Mount speaks about that which masters our lives and the consequences of that mastery. If I had to pick one verse as a key to Matthew 5–7, it would be Matthew 5:20: "For I say to you, that unless your righteousness surpasses *that* of the scribes and Pharisees, you shall not enter the kingdom of heaven."

The kingdom of heaven implies a realm of rulership. Where there's a kingdom, there's a king! As you worked through your study yesterday, you saw that the King of heaven is none other than our heavenly Father. According to Matthew 5:34, His throne is in heaven.

As you marked every reference to the kingdom or the kingdom of heaven yesterday, one thing you may have noted is that only the righteous will enter the kingdom of heaven — only those who possess a righteousness born from faith in the Righteous One, the Lord Jesus Christ. According to our Lord's words, the poor in spirit and those persecuted for righteousness are among those who inherit the kingdom of heaven. Such people, because they have not only heard the Word of God but obeyed it, have a righteousness that exceeds the righteousness of the scribes and Pharisees (Matthew 5:3, 10, 20; 7:21).

But will it be the same for everyone in the kingdom of heaven?

Will everything and everyone be "equal"?

Not according to Matthew 5:19. Some will be called "least" while others will be called "great." What will make the difference? The degree to which each keeps God's commandments and teaches others respect for them. When I share the gospel, I hear all sorts of reasons why people who live in sin think they are still going to heaven. I also hear people say they aren't really interested in the rewards of godly living. They simply want to "make it into heaven" when life is over.

When I hear such things, I seriously wonder whether these people really know God and His Word. People are woefully ignorant of the fact that the Bible speaks of a day of accounting — for the lost *and* for Christians. Second Corinthians 5:10 and Romans 14:10 remind us of the day of accounting for Christians.

1. Look up 2 Corinthians 5:10 and Romans 14:10 in your Bible. In the space provided, record what you learn about "being recompensed" or rewarded for our deeds. Note carefully the context of these verses; read enough of the surrounding verses to understand who is speaking, to whom, and why.

2. Read again the two passages printed below.

"But lay up for yourselves treasures in heaven, where neither moth nor rust destroys, and where thieves do not break in or steal." (Matthew 6:20)

"Rejoice, and be glad, for your reward in heaven is great, for so they persecuted the prophets who were before you." (Matthew 5:12)

It is apparent from these verses that we can lay up treasures in heaven and that there will be rewards. What possible relationship do you see between these two verses and the judgment seat of Christ?

Have you ever thought about all this before — your accountability to God even as a Christian? Have you considered that you could miss certain rewards or treasures because you did not walk in obedience and dedication?

Sobering thoughts aren't they? When I first heard about the judgment seat of Christ, I didn't like it! I wanted to believe that heaven would be the same for every child of God. As I have studied, however, I've seen that this isn't true! There are those who will be "least" and those who will be "greatest" in the kingdom of heaven!

Whenever I teach 2 Corinthians 5:10 — that every Christian will "appear before the judgment seat of Christ, that each one may be recompensed for his deeds in the body, according to what he has done, whether good or bad" — one of the first things my students ask is, "What about our sins? Are we going to be judged for our sins?"

My answer to this question is no.

Jesus was judged for our sins when God "made Him who knew no sin *to be* sin on our behalf" (2 Corinthians 5:21). Since Jesus purged us from our sins, "having offered one sacrifice for sins for all time," there is therefore "no condemnation for those who are in Christ Jesus" (Hebrews 1:3; 10:12; Romans 8:1). We cannot be judged for what Jesus has already paid for!

However, when a Christian walks in sin for a period of time, that time is lost as far as being profitable for the glory of God and His kingdom. It is wasted, for "apart from Me [Him] you can do nothing" (John 15:5). This, I believe, brings a resulting loss of reward.

While we are on the subject, let's look at one more passage which deals with a Christian's accountability. Read 1 Corinthians 3:10–15, printed below, and answer the questions that follow.

According to the grace of God which was given to me, as a wise master builder I laid a foundation, and another is building upon it. But let each man be careful how he builds upon it. For no man can lay a foundation other than the one which is laid, which is Jesus Christ. Now if any man builds upon the foundation with gold, silver, precious stones, wood, hay, straw, each man's work will become evident; for the day will show it, because it is *to be* revealed with fire; and the fire itself will test the quality of each man's work. If any man's work which he has built upon it remains, he shall receive a reward. If any man's work is burned up, he shall suffer loss; but he himself shall be saved, yet so as through fire.

1. What is the foundation?

2. What types of materials are used for building upon this foundation?

3. What is to be tested — and how?

4. What happens to the man…
    a. whose work is burned up?

    b. whose work abides?

Because of its context, I believe this passage in 1 Corinthians 3 is primarily an admonition to teachers. But there is certainly a wider application here as well. Paul is warning all of us about our accountability to our Lord. His message? *Be careful how you build.*

Basically there are two types of "building materials": those which can be produced by man — wood, hay, and straw — and that which already exists but must be discovered by man — gold, silver, and precious stones. God created the latter when He made the earth. Man only discovers and appropriates what is already there. But wood, hay, and straw are the fruits of man's labor. They are temporal and can be destroyed by fire.

What is God saying in all of this? Simply that whatever man produces in and of himself, apart from God, has no eternal value; he will not receive a reward for it. However, the work that comes through us because of God has great and eternal value. It is worthy of reward.

When it comes to explaining the Judgment Seat of Christ — the rewards for the deeds done in our body — I feel like a child in my comprehension of it. Yet inadequate as our understanding may be, Beloved, judgment will surely come to pass because it is written in His unchangeable Word. Therefore, I want to live in the light of it. What about you? Would doing so change the way you are living? If so, how? Think about it, write it out below…and then live accordingly!

The rewards may last forever.

DAY   THREE

The theme of Jesus' sermon is the righteous lifestyle of those who belong to His kingdom. It makes sense, then, that we ought to learn as much as we can about the kingdom of heaven.

When you study all the references to the kingdom of heaven, you see that the term is used basically in four different ways. Let me give them to you:

THE FOUR ASPECTS OF THE KINGDOM OF HEAVEN

1. *God's literal abiding place in the third heaven.* In 2 Corinthians 12, Paul speaks of being caught up to this place. This is God's dwelling place, the place of His throne as described in Revelation 4–5. It is where redeemed people go at their death.

2. *God's universal and eternal dominion over the heavens,* including all its angelic host, good and evil, and over the earth.

3. *The invisible spiritual rulership of Jesus Christ within the lives of those who have genuinely been born again of the Spirit of God.* This aspect of the kingdom began with Jesus' first coming and continues as men believe on and receive the Lord Jesus Christ as their redeemer.

4. *Jesus' reign over the whole earth* at which time all other kingdoms are banished. Although there is debate among theologians and their followers, many believe this kingdom will last for a literal millennium which will begin at Christ's second coming to earth and continue for one thousand years on the earth as we know it now…and then take us into eternity.

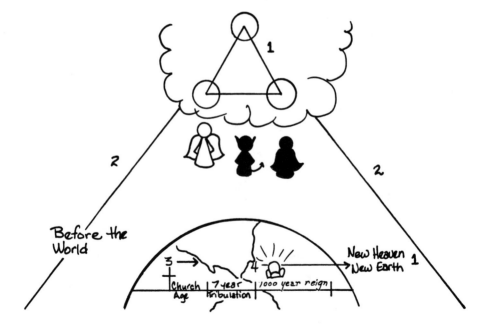

For the sake of clarity, examine the simple graphic on the previous page, matching the numbers with those just given. The drawing may help you to gain a sense of time and place in these mysterious matters.

This is enough information to absorb in one day. Tomorrow we will begin a progressive study of each aspect of the kingdom of heaven. In the meantime, review what you have learned.

As you read about different aspects of the kingdom of heaven, where did you find yourself in relationship to each one? Could you relate to any of them? Has God ever taken up His residence as King in your life? Have you ever prayed that prayer commonly called "The Lord's Prayer"? If so, did you truly mean it? Do you long for His kingdom to come, for His will to be done on earth even as it is done in heaven? These are good things to stop and meditate upon.

D A Y   F O U R

Have you ever stretched out flat on your back in the grass on a warm summer day and gazed at the heavens? Have you ever found yourself wondering what it's like beyond that deep blue dome of sky? Or have you ever flown above the clouds, with the earth obscured from your view, and felt drawn to go even higher and higher — to see God? Sometimes I've gazed into a clear night sky, dazzled by the brilliance of stars cast like diamonds on black velvet, thinking of the time when Jesus will come to take me home.

Home! Heaven! What is it like where God is? Mark every reference to God in yellow or with a ⟨God⟩ Then, with another color or symbol, mark every reference to ⟨△⟩ God's throne. Also mark any reference to the Spirit. I mark references to the Holy Spirit like this ⟨SPIRIT⟩ using one side of the triangle that represents God. Also, I high-light it in yellow. All this marking and coloring simply serve as learning tools to help us focus in, absorb, and remember what we are reading.

Revelation 4 and 5 give the best description I know of. Let's take some time, then, to read these two awesome chapters. As you read Revelation 4, printed out for you, try to get a mental picture of what is described. Then, at the end of the chapter, either list everything you learn about God's dwelling place or draw a simple diagram of what you have read.

Now wait a minute! Before you laugh at the last suggestion because you don't consider yourself an artist, let me tell you what has happened as a result of Precept Ministries' four-part inductive study of Revelation. The students actually draw (everything from line drawings and stick figures to more elaborate works of "art") all the events of Revelation. Some begin kicking and screaming — but end up saying it was the most beneficial activity they had ever done, for now they can see the book in their "mind's eye."

So give it a try…nobody has to see your work, unless of course you want to show it to them.

If you choose to do the drawing, rather than simply listing what you observed, don't crowd your picture. You'll want to add a few more elements after reading Revelation 5.

➤ REVELATION 4

¹ After these things I looked, and behold, a door *standing* open in heaven, and the first voice which I had heard, like *the sound* of a trumpet speaking with me, said, "Come up here, and I will show you what must take place after these things."

² Immediately I was in the Spirit; and behold, a throne was standing in heaven, and One sitting on the throne.

³ And He who was sitting *was* like a jasper stone and a sardius in appearance; and *there was* a rainbow around the throne, like an emerald in appearance.

⁴ And around the throne *were* twenty-four thrones; and upon the thrones I *saw* twenty-four elders sitting, clothed in white garments, and golden crowns on their heads.

⁵ And from the throne proceed flashes of lightning and sounds and peals of thunder. And *there were* seven lamps of fire burning before the throne, which are the seven Spirits of God;

6 and before the throne *there was*, as it were, a sea of glass like crystal; and in the center and around the throne, four living creatures full of eyes in front and behind.

7 And the first creature *was* like a lion, and the second creature like a calf, and the third creature had a face like that of a man, and the fourth creature *was* like a flying eagle.

8 And the four living creatures, each one of them having six wings, are full of eyes around and within; and day and night they do not cease to say,

"HOLY, HOLY, HOLY, is THE LORD GOD, THE ALMIGHTY, who was and who is and who is to come."

9 And when the living creatures give glory and honor and thanks to Him who sits on the throne, to Him who lives forever and ever,

10 the twenty-four elders will fall down before Him who sits on the throne, and will worship Him who lives forever and ever, and will cast their crowns before the throne, saying,

11 "Worthy art Thou, our Lord and our God, to receive glory and honor and power; for Thou didst create all things, and because of Thy will they existed, and were created."

Now that you have completed Revelation 4, let's finish by doing the same with Revelation 5. Continue to mark chapter 5 as you did chapter 4. This time, however, you will also want to mark every reference to the Lord Jesus Christ, including all pronouns and synonyms. I mark Jesus with a symbol like this   JESUS\   and highlight it in yellow. Also, as you read

Revelation 5, carefully note *who* is singing the first new song and about *whom* they are singing besides Jesus. To whom does the pronoun "them" refer in the new song?

➤ REVELATION 5

1 And I saw in the right hand of Him who sat on the throne a book written inside and on the back, sealed up with seven seals.

2 And I saw a strong angel proclaiming with a loud voice, "Who is worthy to open the book and to break its seals?"

3 And no one in heaven, or on the earth, or under the earth, was able to open the book, or to look into it.

4 And I *began* to weep greatly, because no one was found worthy to open the book, or to look into it;

5 and one of the elders said to me, "Stop weeping; behold, the Lion that is from the tribe of Judah, the Root of David, has overcome so as to open the book and its seven seals."

6 And I saw between the throne (with the four living creatures) and the elders a Lamb standing, as if slain, having seven horns and seven eyes, which are the seven Spirits of God, sent out into all the earth.

7 And He came and took *it* out of the right hand of Him who sat on the throne.

8 And when He had taken the book, the four living creatures and the twenty-four elders fell down before the Lamb, having each one a harp, and golden bowls full of incense, which are the prayers of the saints.

9 And they sang a new song, saying,

"Worthy art Thou to take the book, and to break its seals; for Thou wast slain, and didst purchase for God with Thy blood *men* from every tribe and tongue and people and nation.

10 "And Thou has made them *to be* a kingdom and priests to our God; and they will reign upon the earth."

11 And I looked, and I heard the voice of many angels around the throne and the living creatures and the elders; and the number of them was myriads of myriads, and thousands of thousands,

12 saying with a loud voice,

> "Worthy is the Lamb that was slain to receive power and riches and wisdom and might and honor and glory and blessing."

13 And every created thing which is in heaven and on the earth and under the earth and on the sea, and all things in them, I heard saying,

> "To Him who sits on the throne, and to the Lamb, *be* blessing and honor and glory and dominion forever and ever."

14 And the four living creatures kept saying, "Amen." And the elders fell down and worshiped.

Now, Beloved, why don't you get on your knees or on your face before God and spend some time simply worshiping Him, joining those around the throne saying, "Worthy art Thou, our Lord and our God, to receive glory and honor and power; for Thou didst create all things, and because of Thy will they existed, and were created" (Revelation 4:11).

When you rise to go about your duties, remember, my friend, you exist because God willed it. You were created for His pleasure. Take Him at His word on this! Believe and feel the high value God has placed upon you. And then live accordingly! Refuse to believe Satan's lies.

Now…worship the Lamb:

> "Worthy art Thou to take the book, and to break its seals; for Thou wast slain, and didst purchase for God with Thy blood *men* from every tribe and tongue and people and nation. And Thou hast made them *to be* a kingdom and priests to our God; and they will reign upon the earth." (Revelation 5:9–10)

DAY FIVE

The apostle Paul longed for heaven. His heart's desire was "to depart and be with Christ," the One for whom he had suffered the loss of all things, counting them but rubbish (Philippians 1:23; 3:8). He groaned, longing "to be absent from the body and to be at home with the Lord" (2 Corinthians 5:8).

"At home with the Lord"!

That's where we said Caron is. Where is "at home with the Lord"? Paul says it's in the third heaven, paradise (2 Corinthians 12:2–4).

Is it through the empty space in the north of the heavens (Job 26:7)? It could be! Wherever it is, I know home is where God is!

What security this brings when things on this earth seem so temporal — and so shaky! God's children have a New Jerusalem awaiting them, a heavenly city where they will dwell forever in the very presence of God and His Son.

Let's take a closer look at our eternal city and see what we can learn for ourselves. There's nothing, beloved student, like seeing and studying God's Word for yourself. It's a discipline which will literally transform you more and more into His likeness because His Word is alive — powerful — sharper than any two-edged sword — a discerner of the thoughts and intents — the milk by which we grow — the meat of the mature. I commend you, my friend, for disciplining yourself for the purpose of godliness. You'll never be sorry. On the contrary, you will deeply regret it if you don't.

Now then…

1. Open your Bible, and read Revelation 21:1–22:5. Note who is speaking, who is referred to in this passage, what you learn about them, what this passage is about, what is described, where it is, how it looks, etc. You might want to list your observations below:

Who are those mentioned?

How are they described?

Where will they be?

The New Jerusalem: Where is it?

When will it appear?

What will it be like?

Who will be in it? Who will relate to it?

2. List the five things that impressed you the most from this passage of Scripture.

The New Jerusalem is the eternal destiny of every true child of God. It is as certain as God Himself, therefore:

See to it that you do not refuse Him who is speaking. For if those did not escape when they refused him who warned *them* on earth, much less *shall* we *escape* who turn away from Him who *warns* from heaven. And His voice shook the earth then, but now He has promised, saying, "YET ONCE MORE I WILL SHAKE NOT ONLY THE EARTH, BUT ALSO THE HEAVEN." And this *expression*, "Yet once more," denotes the removing of those things which can be shaken, as of created things, in order that those things which cannot be shaken may remain. Therefore, since we receive a kingdom which cannot be shaken, let us show gratitude, by which we may offer to God an acceptable service with reverence and awe; for our God is a consuming fire. (Hebrews 12:25–29)

O Beloved…if you should die, would you find yourself in heaven, in the presence of God Himself…or in hell? Believe it or not, there are only two destinations at death — and once death comes, your destination is set.

Think about it.

The Coming Glory of His Kingdom

I n 1983, millions of Americans sat by television sets to watch "The Day After," a television production that dealt with the results of a nuclear holocaust. Special interviews followed as "experts" discussed the purpose for such a program, the probabilities for such an event, and what effect "The Day After" might have on those who viewed it.

In all the discussions no one ever considered the fact that there is a God who sits in the heavens controlling the affairs of mankind. Never once did anyone mention that there is a God who is in control of history and that what was proposed in "The Day After" did not mesh with the Bible's account of God's plans for the future.

The prophet Amos wrote, "Surely the Lord GOD does nothing unless He reveals His secret counsel to His servants the prophets" (3:7). And it is His servants the prophets who have recorded for us the processes by which God will bring the kingdoms of this world into submission under His kingdom.

For the most part — and increasingly so — mankind remains ignorant of God's universal dominion over the heavens and the earth. This is as true today as in the ancient time of King Nebuchadnezzar. How well Nebuchadnezzar's story illustrates God's sovereign rule over the universe from His throne in heaven.

You will find it in Daniel, chapter 4.

As you read this chapter in your Bible, note how God gets Nebuchadnezzar's attention with His own "late night special." Observe how the proud king ignores what is told him, thinking he can escape the just judgment of God. Then watch carefully how God proves Himself to be God, finally gaining Nebuchadnezzar's full attention and respect. As you read, you might want to mark every reference to the "Most High."

When you finish, look back at verses 34–35 of Daniel 4. List below "where" God accomplishes His will — or, to put it another way, the realm of His rulership.

If you have studied our earlier text on the Sermon on the Mount, *Lord, Only You Can Change Me*, you know what assurance these verses have brought to my life…and I trust to yours also. As you look up Daniel 4:34–35, compare what you learn here with the chart on page 13 of our first week of study.

God taught Nebuchadnezzar a hard, humbling, but worthwhile lesson he would never forget. There had never been an empire like Babylon. The only problem was that Nebuchadnezzar thought he had built Babylon by the might of his own power and for the glory of his own majesty (Daniel 4:30). He forgot that there is a God in heaven who changes the times and the epochs, who removes kings and establishes kings, who gives kingdoms, power, strength, and glory (Daniel 2:21, 37). Therefore, God had to teach Nebuchadnezzar a lesson so he would recognize "that the Most High is ruler over the realm of mankind, and bestows it on whomever He wishes" (Daniel 4:32).

Through God's chastening but gracious hand, Nebuchadnezzar came to his senses. He saw clearly that God's kingdom is the supreme kingdom, ruling over all others — whether they be visible or invisible, earthly or spiritual.

God is in charge. He's the Master, and if He's yours, you need not worry about "The Day After." Seek first His kingdom and His righteousness, and He'll shelter you in the hollow of His hand. No one will pluck you out. You will have an eternal place in His kingdom. Study His book. It has the whole story recorded from beginning to end.

D A Y   T W O

Can you and I know now, for certain, that the kingdom of heaven is ours? Our sure possession?

As you read the beatitudes in Matthew 5:3–12, it's interesting to note that most of the beatitudes are associated with the future tense. Those who mourn, for example, *will be* comforted. The gentle or meek *shall inherit* the earth. But not every reference is tied to the future. In verse 3 Jesus says, "Blessed are the poor in spirit for theirs *is* the kingdom of heaven." And in verse 10 He tells us, "Blessed are those who have been persecuted for the sake of righteousness, for theirs *is* the kingdom of heaven."

When Jesus refers to entering the kingdom of heaven in the Sermon on the Mount, obviously He is not talking about it in the sense of its universal dominion. His reference is to belonging right now to His spiritual, invisible kingdom which will some day guarantee entrance into the third heaven of God's throne.

Our task today, therefore, is to take a careful look at the kingdom of heaven (or the kingdom of God, as it is sometimes called) to which only the redeemed of Jesus Christ belong.

Let's begin with the familiar story of the rich young ruler in Mark 10:17–27. As you read, mark every reference to eternal life and the kingdom of God in the same way. For instance, you may want to underline it, highlight it in a certain color, or draw a little crown above each reference, like this: ⌒⌒ . Marking the text, remember, is a learning device which helps you observe the text more accurately and better retain what you are seeing.

➤ MARK 10:17-27

17 And as He was setting out on a journey, a man ran up to Him and knelt before Him, and *began* asking Him, "Good Teacher, what shall I do to inherit eternal life?"

18 And Jesus said to him, "Why do you call Me good? No one is good except God alone.

19 "You know the commandments, 'DO NOT MURDER, DO NOT COMMIT ADULTERY, DO NOT STEAL, DO NOT BEAR FALSE WITNESS, Do not defraud, HONOR YOUR FATHER AND MOTHER.'"

20 And he said to Him, "Teacher, I have kept all these things from my youth up."

21 And looking at him, Jesus felt a love for him, and said to him, "One thing you lack: go and sell all you possess, and give to the poor, and you shall have treasure in heaven; and come, follow Me."

22 But at these words his face fell, and he went away grieved, for he was one who owned much property.

23 And Jesus, looking around, said to His disciples, "How hard it will be for those who are wealthy to enter the kingdom of God!"

24 And the disciples were amazed at His words. But Jesus answered again and said to them, "Children, how hard it is to enter the kingdom of God!

25 "It is easier for a camel to go through the eye of a needle than for a rich man to enter the kingdom of God!"

26 And they were even more astonished and said to Him, "Then who can be saved?"

27 Looking upon them, Jesus said, "With men it is impossible, but not with God; for all things are possible with God."

Now then, diligent one, answer the questions that follow. The very processing of verbalizing and writing out answers will help you remember what you are studying. It is all part of the vital learning process.

1. What did the young man want to know?

2. Look at Jesus' interesting response in verse 18. Why do you think Jesus challenged this young man on the way he addressed Him? Was Jesus trying to make him recognize something about Himself?

3. What were Jesus' instructions?

4. If the young man had chosen to obey the Lord and follow, what would he have gained?

5. How did the young man respond?

6. What did the young man lack? How did he respond to Jesus' instructions regarding this "one thing"?

7. Open your Bible and read Exodus 20:1–17, where the Ten Commandments are listed. Did the young man's actions show disregard for any of the commandments? If so, which one and in what way?

8. Summarize what you learn from this passage in Mark 10 about the kingdom of heaven or kingdom of God.

The young man wanted eternal life, yet he never entered the kingdom of God because he wanted it on his own terms! He loved his riches more than he loved God! I say that because the first time Jesus quoted the commandments, He deliberately skipped over the first and foremost commandment — "Thou shalt have no other gods before me" and "thou shalt love the Lord thy God with all thy heart, and with all thy soul, and with all thy mind, and with all thy strength..." (Exodus 20:3; Mark 12:30, KJV). Little did the young man realize that this was the one commandment he had *not* kept. Not until Jesus told him to sell all that he had and follow Him did his idol become visible. Riches superseded God!

"Jesus felt a love for him," but He could not let him enter His kingdom. The way is narrow, the gate small, and the those who enter His kingdom are few. Isn't that what we read in Matthew 7 in the first week of our study?

Now, Beloved, we must not simply read Scripture, without examining our beliefs and our lifestyle in the light of what we are learning from the Word. So let me ask you a few questions.

What is your relationship with Jesus Christ?

Do you want the kingdom of heaven — now? On whose terms can you have it?

Who must be your God...your Master?

Is there anything keeping you from forsaking all to follow Him?

Is it worth missing the kingdom?

I urge you, my friend, to give these things serious thought.

D A Y   T H R E E

On Day One we did a brief study of God's kingdom from the aspect of His universal dominion. Yesterday we looked at the kingdom as it pertains to those who are saved and are sons and daughters of the kingdom. They belong to His invisible, spiritual kingdom — known to God, but not necessarily recognized by man.

Matthew 13 highlights both of these aspects of God's kingdom in the parable of the wheat and the tares.

Read Matthew 13:24–30, 36–43, and note carefully the references to the two aspects of the kingdom. As you read, mark every reference to the kingdom as you have done previously. Also, note the contrast between the wheat and the tares. I'd suggest you mark the references to the wheat and the tares in distinctive ways so you can easily spot them in the text.

➤ MATTHEW 13:24–30, 36–43

24 He presented another parable to them, saying, "The kingdom of heaven may be compared to a man who sowed good seed in his field.

25 "But while men were sleeping, his enemy came and sowed tares [a weed resembling wheat] also among the wheat, and went away.

26 "But when the wheat sprang up and bore grain, then the tares became evident also.

27 "And the slaves of the landowner came and said to him, 'Sir, did you not sow good seed in your field? How then does it have tares?'

28 "And he said to them, 'An enemy has done this!' And the slaves said to him, 'Do you want us, then, to go and gather them up?'

29 "But he said, 'No; lest while you are gathering up the tares, you may also root up the wheat with them.

30 'Allow both to grow together until the harvest; and in the time of the harvest I will say to the reapers, "First gather up the tares and bind them in bundles to burn them up; but gather the wheat into my barn."'"

36 Then He left the multitudes, and went into the house. And His disciples came to Him, saying, "Explain to us the parable of the tares of the field."

37 And He answered and said, "The one who sows the good seed is the Son of Man,

38 and the field is the world; and *as for* the good seed, these are the sons of the kingdom; and the tares are the sons of the evil *one;*

39 and the enemy who sowed them is the devil, and the harvest is the end of the age; and the reapers are angels.

40 "Therefore just as the tares are gathered up and burned with fire, so shall it be at the end of the age.

41 "The Son of Man will send forth His angels, and they will gather out of His kingdom all stumbling blocks, and those who commit lawlessness,

42 and will cast them into the furnace of fire; in that place there shall be weeping and gnashing of teeth.

43 "Then THE RIGHTEOUS WILL SHINE FORTH AS THE SUN in the kingdom of their Father. He who has ears, let him hear."

1. Who are the wheat? What did you learn about them from marking the text?

2. Who are the tares?

3. From where are the tares gathered?

4. What is done to the tares?

5. What happens to the righteous (wheat)?

6. Who are the reapers?

7. When does all this happen?

It's interesting, isn't it, that "the wheat" are referred to as righteous! Do you see how this parallels the Sermon on the Mount, which clearly teaches that only the righteous will inherit the kingdom of heaven?

Are you wheat or tares? You know, it's very hard to distinguish the two until fruit-bearing time comes. Only by their fruit can you really distinguish which is which. What does the fruit of your life bear witness to? Wheat or tares? Talk to God about it.

As you do, however, let me give you two cautions. First, don't allow yourself, Beloved, to be unjustly condemned by the accuser of the brethren who would have you doubt a salvation you genuinely possess. God knows who are His. His Spirit will not only bear witness with your spirit, but He has also given you the short epistle of 1 John that you might inspect your own fruit and see if it gives evidence of true salvation. On the other hand (and here is the second caution), don't allow the enemy to deceive you into thinking you have salvation when you really don't! Walking down an aisle, being baptized, being born into a Christian family, joining a church, or making a public "profession" of faith is no guarantee of your salvation. Good as these things might be, they are not that which saves you! Salvation comes only through a relationship with the Lord Jesus Christ, a relationship that makes you a new creature and produces righteousness.

DAY   FOUR

Jesus' first coming inaugurated His invisible spiritual reign within the hearts of mankind. The King had come and with Him, His kingdom.

Yet the kingdom he brought did not meet the Jews' expectations.

They wanted that *visible* kingdom where Messiah would deliver Israel from the bondage of her oppressors, where Messiah would sit upon His throne ruling with a rod of iron, where all nations would come yearly to Jerusalem to give homage to the Jewish Messiah.

In his gospel, Matthew takes his Jewish readers from the invisible kingdom to the visible kingdom, from salvation to the Millennium, showing how King Jesus fulfills the Law and the Prophets by bringing the kingdom of heaven to earth.

The purpose of Matthew's Gospel was to present Jesus as Messiah and King. Matthew wanted to show that Jesus the King had come — and therefore the kingdom of heaven was at hand. For this reason, Matthew is very careful to show us how Jesus fulfills the Old Testament promise of a king and a kingdom. This is why Matthew takes Jesus' genealogy back to Abraham, so we can see that Jesus is the seed promised to Abraham. Therefore, He is the Christ (the Messiah).

The word *kingdom* is used fifty-six times in Matthew — more than in any of the other gospels. The first reference is Matthew 3:2, and the last is Matthew 26:29. The word *king* is used twenty-three times. The first reference is Matthew 1:6, where Matthew is very careful to show Jesus' genealogy through David. From the tribe of Judah and the line of David would come the One who was to rule over all the earth. The last reference to the king is Matthew 27:42, where we read that the priests, the scribes, and the elders mockingly said, "He is the King of Israel." Of the first eight words of Matthew's gospel, four of those are *Jesus* — *Christ* — *David* — *Abraham*. Who else could be the Messiah, the King, to establish the kingdom of God?

It is interesting to note that Matthew gives Jesus' legal descent through Joseph, showing His right to rule. Luke gives Jesus' descent through his mother, Mary. Both genealogies include Abraham and David. In his *Survey of the New Testament*, Irving Jensen gives a beautiful outline of the Gospel of Matthew. Let me share it with you.

Matthew 1:1–4:11
The King's Presentation
Behold Him

Matthew 4:12–16:20
The King's Proclamation
Understand Him

Matthew 16:21–28:20
The King's Passion
Follow Him

Jesus' message in Matthew 4:17 is "Repent, for the kingdom of heaven is at hand." Salvation had come at last. Here was the Lamb of God, who would take away the sin of the world. Here was the One who would begin His reign in the hearts of men although His time had not come to reign upon the earth.

Matthew 12:28 shows us the same truth. "But if I cast out demons by the Spirit of God, then the kingdom of God has come upon you." Had the kingdom of God come? Yes, it had come. Its coming at this point was spiritual and invisible, yet there was no denying it because He was casting out demons by the Spirit of God. The spirit world recognized His kingship and had to obey!

In Matthew 24 and 25, Jesus tells His disciples of His second coming, the time when He will set up His throne and begin His visible reign upon the earth. It would be wonderful and enlightening if you would read all of

Matthew 24–25 in your Bible. However, if there is not time, then read what we have printed out. As you read, mark every reference to the coming of the Son of Man (Jesus) with a ⌒⌒⌒⌒ like this. Also, mark every reference to time or the passage of time with a little clock like this (For instance, you would draw a clock above the phrase "of those days.")

➤ MATTHEW 24:29–31

29 "But immediately after the tribulation of those days THE SUN WILL BE DARKENED, AND THE MOON WILL NOT GIVE ITS LIGHT, AND THE STARS WILL FALL FROM THE SKY, and the powers of the heavens will be shaken,

30 and then the sign of the Son of Man will appear in the sky, and then all the tribes of the earth will mourn, and they will see the SON OF MAN COMING IN THE CLOUDS OF THE SKY with power and great glory.

31 "And He will send forth His angels with A GREAT TRUMPET and THEY WILL GATHER TOGETHER His elect from the four winds, from one end of the sky to the other."

➤ MATTHEW 25:31–46

31 "But when the Son of Man comes in His glory, and all the angels with Him, then he will sit on His glorious throne.

32 "And all the nations will be gathered before Him; and He will separate them from one another, as the shepherd separates the sheep from the goats;

33 and He will put the sheep on His right, and the goats on His left.

34 "Then the King will say to those on His right, 'Come, you who are blessed of My Father, inherit the kingdom prepared for you from the foundation of the world.

35 'For I was hungry, and you gave Me *something* to eat; I was thirsty, and you gave Me drink; I was a stranger, and you invited Me in;

36 naked, and you clothed Me; I was sick, and you visited Me; I was in prison, and you came to Me.'

37 "Then the righteous will answer Him, saying, 'Lord, when did we see You hungry, and feed You, or thirsty, and give You drink?

38 'And when did we see You a stranger, and invite You in, or naked, and clothe You?

39 'And when did we see You sick, or in prison, and come to You?'

40 "And the King will answer and say to them, 'Truly I say to you, to the extent that you did it to one of these brothers of Mine, *even* the least *of them*, you did it to Me.'

41 "Then He will also say to those on His left, 'Depart from Me, accursed ones, into the eternal fire which has been prepared for the devil and his angels;

42 for I was hungry, and you gave Me *nothing* to eat; I was thirsty, and you gave Me nothing to drink;

43 I was a stranger, and you did not invite Me in; naked, and you did not clothe Me; sick, and in prison, and you did not visit Me.'

44 "Then they themselves also will answer, saying, 'Lord, when did we see You hungry, or thirsty, or a stranger, or naked, or sick, or in prison, and did not take care of You?'

45 "Then He will answer them, saying, 'Truly I say to you, to the extent that you did not do it to one of the least of these, you did not do it to Me.'

46 "And these will go away into eternal punishment, but the righteous into eternal life."

1. Who is going to come on the clouds of the sky with great power and great glory? Note what He is called.

2. Now, compare that title with Daniel 7:13–14. Who was given dominion, glory, and a kingdom "that all the peoples, nations, and men of every language might serve Him"?

3. According to Matthew 24:29–30, when will this occur?

4. Who will see it happen?

5. How does Matthew 25:31 parallel Matthew 24:29–30? Read the verses carefully, noting the similarities and listing them below.

6. In Matthew 25:31–40 the Son of Man comes to sit on His glorious throne. In Matthew 25:34 what title does this Son of Man bear?

7. What does He offer those sheep whom He puts on His right?

8. Do you think this passage speaks of a spiritual kingdom or a literal kingdom? Why?

9. According to Matthew 25:37, what does He call those on His right?

10. How does the above description fit with the description of those in the Sermon on the Mount who inherit the kingdom of heaven and the earth?

Beloved, Jesus is coming again. We do not know the day, the hour, or the year, but we can know with absolute certainty that Jesus will come to reign as King of kings and Lord of lords. The secret of the zeal of the early church was that they lived as if He might come at any time. They knew that their citizenship was in heaven (Philippians 3:20).

Let me leave you with one question to meditate upon. How similar is your life to those in Thessalonica who "turned to God from idols to serve a living and true God, and to wait for His Son from heaven, whom he raised from the dead, *that is* Jesus, who delivers us from the wrath to come" (1 Thessalonians 1:9–10)?

D A Y   F I V E

Some think that the Sermon on the Mount describes a lifestyle that is impossible to live except in "the kingdom age." To many "the kingdom age" is synonymous with the Millennium, the thousand-year reign of Jesus Christ upon earth.

Possibly some of you are like me. I wasn't saved until I was twenty-nine. I had never even heard about Jesus Christ returning to earth and setting up a literal kingdom. I must admit that when I heard about prophecy and began a study of it, I was so excited I didn't want to study anything else.

That happens to a lot of us, doesn't it?

Now, in all fairness, I want to remind you again that some Christians do not believe in a literal, millennial kingdom where Jesus Christ will rule and reign for a thousand years. They are called amillennialists, the "a" before the word *millennium* denoting "without."

There are some who believe the Sermon on the Mount presents such a lofty lifestyle that it couldn't possibly be for us today. These would believe it must refer to the lifestyle of those living during the millennial reign of our Lord Jesus Christ.

Are they right?

Is the Sermon on the Mount for then…or for today?

Those who hold that the Sermon on the Mount is for the kingdom age, the Millennium, have basically a twofold reason. Let me share it.

First, they believe that the Gospel of Matthew was directed to the Jews.

Second, they believe that the lifestyle called for in the Sermon is *impossible*. They believe it can be lived only by those who are no longer encumbered by their sinful flesh.

Let's examine this view. We know several things about the Millennium. We know Jesus Christ will rule as King of kings. We know that He will rule with a rod of iron; He will allow no disobedience whatsoever. We know also we will rule with Him. In the light of the truths we know about the Millennium, we need to examine the Sermon on the Mount to see if it could possibly pertain to the Millennium. The answer, I believe, is found within the Sermon itself.

Matthew 5:5 says that the meek *shall* (future tense) inherit the earth. At the time of the Millennium, we will already have inherited the earth, right? Therefore, poverty of spirit (which gives us the kingdom) and meekness (which will give us the earth) would have to occur in our lives *prior* to this time.

Keeping this in mind, let's reason together. If I have already inherited the earth, would I, during the Millennium, be persecuted for the sake of righteousness? Of course not! And yet Matthew 5:10–11 says: "Blessed are those who have been persecuted for the sake of righteousness.... Blessed are you when *men* cast insults at you, and persecute you, and say all kinds of evil against you falsely, on account of Me." Will the saints be persecuted and insulted when Jesus Christ comes in all of His glory to reign over the earth and we rule and reign with Him? No!

The Sermon on the Mount, then, cannot refer to the Millennium.

Let me show you another reason why the Sermon on the Mount is for today rather than the Millennium. Matthew 5:39–41 talks about turning the other cheek when someone slaps you on the cheek, about men's being able to force you to go one mile, about loving your enemies and those who persecute you. During the Millennium will the children of God be slapped about, forced to go a mile, and persecuted by their enemies? No! Therefore, the Sermon on the Mount does not belong to the kingdom age.

There are other views on the Sermon on the Mount we will have to leave for those who want to study the subject "precept upon precept." (See the back of this book for information.) Here is the question we must deal with right now: Is the Sermon on the Mount for today? For if it is, then we would do well to embrace all it teaches.

Personally, I believe it is a must for today. In *The Sermon on the Mount: A Foundation for Understanding,* Bible scholar Robert A. Guelich states:

> As did his predecessors, Augustine viewed the Sermon to be "the perfect measure of the Christian life" and "filled with all the precepts by which the Christian life is formed." For him, the Sermon applied to all Christians and was without question applicable to life.

The Sermon on the Mount is not a new law or an impossible standard to be reached for but never obtained until the Millennium. Rather, it is a teaching given by Jesus Himself on the new relationship with Him that is ours through the New Covenant, salvation by grace through faith.

The first seven beatitudes (Matthew 5:3–9) show the *character* of those who enter into this relationship. The next two beatitudes (verses 10–12) show the *conflict* that such character brings in a world that does not recognize Jesus' lordship. The remainder of the Sermon (5:13–7:27) shows the *conduct* of those who belong to Jesus. This conduct, then, demonstrates the presence of God's sovereign rulership in the life of the child of God, and it is that conduct that you and I are going to study in this book.

So, what is our outline of the Sermon on the Mount? Let me drop one as a plumb line for our study.

THE RIGHTEOUS LIFESTYLE OF THOSE WHO BELONG TO THE KINGDOM OF HEAVEN

Matthew 5:1–2	Prologue
Matthew 5:3–9	Their Character
Matthew 5:10–12	Their Conflict
Matthew 5:13–7:27	Their Conduct
Matthew 7:28–29	Epilogue

As we proceed in our study, faithful student, I believe you will see that the Sermon on the Mount is *only* an impossible lifestyle for those who have not bowed their knees to the King nor yielded up the throne of their hearts to His reign as King of kings and Lord of lords!

If you will but bow —

if you will yield —

the kingdom of heaven, in all its fullness

will be yours.

God Himself will lovingly change you and fit you for the kingdom of heaven.

This is why Jesus came.

Now then, do you remember when I told you that the trail would get a little "steep" in these early chapters? The next chapter will be a challenge — no matter what shape you're in! But these are precious, life-changing truths from God's Word, and if you do your study, hang in there, and ask the Lord for help, you will be rewarded. The view at the top of the trail is magnificent! And the Holy Spirit, your own personal Teacher, will walk with you every step of the way!

HOW TO
HAVE A
NEW HEART

DAY ONE

H ave you ever stopped to wonder why humanity cannot achieve peace on this earth?

It's not that we lack brilliant and talented men and women. We have achieved unbelievable and awesome feats in medicine, technology, and science. The world is now linked by an intricate "information super highway" that enables us to tap into almost instant information and communication with the play of our fingers across our computer keyboards. We have organized vast, far-reaching projects of mercy and rehabilitation. There doesn't seem to be a corner of the world we haven't touched. We have sat at peace tables with instant translation and seasoned diplomats and negotiators. The United Nations has gathered nations around the globe under one roof to make us accountable to one another.

Yet, despite all these things, humanity has not changed.

Wars continue to rage. Assassinations cut down our leaders. Racial hatreds, tribal genocide, and ancient suspicions and jealousies continue to spill blood and spread poison across our globe.

Why is that? Will it ever be possible for man to straighten out man?

Will we ever be able to bring peace on earth, to live in good will toward one another?

We have a historical account of man's affairs for the past six thousand years, but peace has yet to be a reality. The question is, will we ever see it?

Is it any wonder that the Sermon on the Mount leads men and women to resurrect from the grave of history their hope of peace? Scales are removed from the eyes of visionaries, and the hearts of leaders once again are aflame with a passion to lead man to greatness. The Sermon on the Mount calls for a lifestyle that brings what all humankind longs for — a kingdom of righteousness upon the earth.

There's only one problem...men and women persist in believing that they can instill the moral, ethical structure of Jesus' *teaching* without installing Jesus as their King.

And that cannot be.

Thinking that the Sermon on the Mount is the solution to the ills of the world, leaders of the social gospel movement have taken the Sermon as their Magna Carta. They have believed that peace could be attained simply by understanding its principles and applying them to their culture.

Years ago when our youngest son, David, was still at home, Jack and I had a growing conviction that God had gifted our son with leadership potential. We decided to take him to see *Gandhi*, the movie about the great leader of India. We sought to use Gandhi's life as a teaching tool, comparing his convictions with biblical principles of leadership.

Revered by millions, Gandhi was truly an extraordinary man among men. Even many who mocked and despised his methods of dealing with the British secretly admired his ability to subdue his natural responses and live on a higher plane than those about him. Embracing the teaching of the Sermon on the Mount, Gandhi practiced turning the other cheek. He believed, lived, and taught that peace could be achieved apart from violence. In so doing, he won the hearts of his downtrodden and oppressed people. He was a man of devotion, of prayer, and of self-denial. A true visionary leader, he changed the course of his nation's history.

There was only one problem. Gandhi could change his people's direction, but he could not change their hearts. The lifestyle to which he called them, then, was impossible.

Whereas Gandhi's followers could take the blows of the British — turning the other cheek, being dragged away bloody and battered — they could not live peacefully among themselves. Soon after achieving independence from their British overlords, they systematically began to destroy each other! They could handle external wars, it seemed, but not internal ones.

Why? Because the natural man's heart is deceitful and desperately wicked.

Gandhi never learned the secret of *transforming* men's hearts. When I watch a good movie, it's my nature to get into the plot all the way. In the scene that showed Gandhi's assassination, I felt a wave of shock and horror sweep over me. I can still see his eyes — the pain, the disbelief. But my horror didn't come just from his being gunned down — that was bad enough. It was the awful realization that this well-meaning man had just stepped into a Christless eternity. Gandhi, who had appreciated Jesus Christ and even sought to follow some of His teachings, went instantly to hell. The kingdom of heaven was not his because he did not do the will of the Father who is in heaven. He did not believe that Jesus Christ was God incarnate — Lord and Master — the Way, the Truth, and the Life — the only means of salvation. Yet someday, before he is consigned to the Lake of Fire, where the worm dies not and the flame is not quenched, he will bow the knee and confess that Jesus Christ is Lord.

Some look at the Sermon and say, "It's an impossible lifestyle. It serves no purpose except to show men their sin."

Others cry, "No, it's another interpretation of the Law. It does not belong to the age of grace. It stands in opposition to Christ's atoning work. Grace would not demand such a lifestyle."

Albert Schweitzer, a brilliant, self-sacrificing man, said that the Sermon on the Mount was merely "interim-ethics" which make one suitable for the kingdom of God. In other words, if we could live it in our own strength, it would hold us until the kingdom of heaven was realized. Ultradispensationalists have said it is not for today but belongs to the kingdom age when Jesus rules on earth for a thousand years. (A dispensation is an era of time when man is tested with respect to a specific revelation of God's will. An ultradispensationalist, then, is one who rigidly adheres to God's working in a specific way during a specific time with specific people.)

Yet, what does the Sermon on the Mount say when we let it speak for itself?

It tells us that kingdom is the present-tense possession of the poor in spirit and the persecuted. It belongs to those whose righteousness exceeds that of the scribes and Pharisees. It is for those who do the will of the Father. This rules out Schweitzer's "interim-ethics." It also shows that the seemingly impossible demands of the Sermon are *possible*. They are possible to those who come to God in poverty of spirit — who take the narrow way, the small gate — and who hear and act upon the words of God. To those who say that the Sermon on the Mount is for the kingdom age, I would answer that when Jesus Christ comes, I will no longer be persecuted for righteousness' sake, nor will I have to turn the other cheek. I won't have to allow men to sue me, or force me to go one mile, for during the Millennium we will rule and reign with Jesus Christ.

Is the Sermon on the Mount an impossible lifestyle? No, Beloved. It is the lifestyle of Jesus Christ, the manifestation of the righteousness of God. It is being perfect as our heavenly Father is perfect. It is possible, because in the New Covenant, the covenant of grace, God gives us a new heart. He puts His Spirit within us, causing us to walk in His statutes and keep His commandments (Ezekiel 36:26–27).

It is true. We cannot straighten out ourselves, but God can! The world can conform us, but only God can *transform* us. O Beloved, how important it is that you realize this as you study the Sermon on the Mount. It is not merely a code of ethics or a lifestyle to which you must try to conform. It is, rather, the outworking of the inward, transforming work of God.

Think upon these things and talk to God about them. Tomorrow we'll begin the process of study so we can understand from the Word of God how God brings about this transformation. This will be a heavy week of study, my friend, but if you'll "hangeth thou in there," you'll receive a great reward of understanding.

The *Chicago Tribune* carried an article quoting historian Will Durant, saying:

> In any generation there may be eight or ten persons who will be alive in the sense of continuing influence three hundred years after. For instance, Plato still lives and Socrates still lives, but in all of western civilization, the person who stands out above all others is Christ. He undoubtedly was the most permanent influence on our thoughts but not on our actions and that's an important modification. Our actions are very seldom Christian but our theology often is. We wish we could behave like Christ.

That's quite a statement, isn't it? Apparently Will Durant respected the teachings of Jesus. He must have felt, however, that they were impossible to put into action. He couldn't make them work! What Durant did not know is that theology can never work apart from God's presence within a man or woman. Genuine Christianity is a matter of the heart — receiving a new heart. Listen to the Word of God; mark each reference to the heart with a ♡ and hear God's diagnosis of the heart of mankind.

➤ G E N E S I S   8 : 2 1

> And the LORD smelled the soothing aroma; and the LORD said to Himself, "I will never again curse the ground on account of man, for the intent of man's heart is evil from his youth; and I will never again destroy every living thing, as I have done."

➤ J E R E M I A H   1 7 : 9

> "The heart is more deceitful than all else
> And is desperately sick;
> Who can understand it?"

Now list below what you learn from these two verses about the condition of man's heart.

Next, read Romans 7:14–24 very carefully. As you read, mark every occurrence of the word *law* if it refers to the law of God (rather than a principle, such as in verse 23). You might want to mark each reference to law like this:

➤ ROMANS 7:14–24

14 For we know that the Law is spiritual; but I am of flesh, sold into bondage to sin.

15 For that which I am doing, I do not understand; for I am not practicing what I *would* like to *do*, but I am doing the very thing I hate.

16 But if I do the very thing I do not wish *to do*, I agree with the Law, *confessing* that it is good.

17 So now, no longer am I the one doing it, but sin which indwells me.

18 For I know that nothing good dwells in me, that is, in my flesh; for the wishing is present in me, but the doing of the good is not.

19 For the good that I wish, I do not do; but I practice the very evil that I do not wish.

20 But if I am doing the very thing I do not wish, I am no longer the one doing it, but sin which dwells in me.

21 I find then the principle that evil is present in me, the one who wishes to do good.

22 For I joyfully concur with the law of God in the inner man,

23 but I see a different law in the members of my body, waging war against the law of my mind, and making me a prisoner of the law of sin which is in my members.

24 Wretched man that I am! Who will set me free from the body of this death?

Now — what do you learn about the Law of God from this passage? Let me ask you several questions.

1. Is there anything *wrong* with the Law? How do you know?

2. Why can't man keep the Law?

3. What is Paul's question in this passage?

Is there any solution — any answer — to Paul's dilemma? Yes, there is, Beloved. God has a way to take care of our deceitful and desperately wicked hearts, a way to handle the sin which indwells us, a way to fulfill the just requirements of the Law. That's what this week's study is all about. Tomorrow, we'll dig a little deeper, my friend. But before I leave you, I just have to take a moment to tell you of the love and gratitude I feel in my heart for you. I know this deep feeling within me is from the Lord, for I don't even know who you are, or how this book will ever come into your hands. Nevertheless, I feel a deep love and sense of gratitude welling up within me as I think about you, my reader. Thank you for being serious about following our Lord. Thank you for wanting to go on to greater maturity. I know study requires great discipline — saying no to other things.

And I also know that it's a battle.

The enemy will do everything he can to keep you from the Word of God — and some of his tactics will have the guise of nobility. He'll do everything he can to keep you so busy, so preoccupied that you don't have time to really dig into the Word. After all, the Word is your shield and your sword, your defensive and offensive weapon against Satan. Is it any wonder that we experience warfare? So I thank you for persevering, for enduring hardship as a good soldier of Jesus Christ, for keeping your priorities straight. May God bless you exceeding abundantly above all that you can ask or think. May our passion be that of Philippians 3:7–14.

> But whatever things were gain to me, those things I have counted as loss for the sake of Christ. More than that, I count all things to be loss in view of the surpassing value of knowing Christ Jesus my Lord, for whom I have suffered the loss of all things, and count them but rubbish in order that I may gain Christ, and may be found in Him, not having a righteousness of my own derived from *the* Law, but that which is through faith in Christ, the righteousness which *comes* from God on the basis of faith, that I may know Him, and the power of His resurrection and the fellowship of His sufferings, being conformed to His death; in order that I may attain to the resurrection from the dead. Not that I have already obtained *it,* or have already become perfect, but I press on in order that I may lay hold of that for which also I was laid hold of by Christ Jesus. Brethren, I do not regard myself as having laid hold of *it* yet; but one thing *I do:* forgetting what *lies* behind and reaching forward to what *lies* ahead, I press on toward the goal for the prize of the upward call of God in Christ Jesus.

DAY THREE

In your study yesterday you saw several things.

You saw that the natural, human heart is deceitful and desperately wicked, even from youth.

You saw that the Law is spiritual; the Law is good. Matthew 5:17 says that Jesus did not come to abolish the Law but to fulfill it. The next verse tells us that "not the smallest letter or stroke shall pass away from the Law, until all is accomplished." The Law gives us God's standard of righteousness. There is nothing wrong with the Law. The problem is us!

Man cannot keep the Law because of the condition of his heart and of his flesh. You saw in Romans 7 that sin dwells in man. Even though man may desire and long to do what the Law says, he is unable to do it because sin dwells in him. As it says in Romans 7:14, we are "of flesh, sold into bondage to sin." Here, then, was the terrible dilemma we saw in yesterday's study: Some men and women truly desire to walk in obedience to the Law but cannot because of the power of sin within them.

Considering these things, you may say, "It makes sense that Christians want to keep God's Law. But what about unbelievers? Can unsaved people desire to be holy — to keep God's Law?" Of course. John Wesley, the founder of Methodism, sought to serve God. He went through all sorts of religious disciplines, and yet it was many years before he realized that salvation is by grace. It was then that he entered into the New Covenant.

The scribes, the Pharisees, the religious Jews of Jesus' day also sought to keep the Law. They realized that it was spiritual and good. The problem was, they had uncircumcised hearts. Their hearts had never been circumcised by the Spirit of God. (Romans 2:29 says "circumcision is that which is of the heart, by the Spirit, not by the letter.") The scribes and Pharisees were trying to deal with their old, sinful hearts by living according to the letter of the Law. They were blind to the teaching of Ezekiel which promised them a new heart.

For the sake of clarity, let's summarize man's problem…and then we will see God's solution. In and of himself, man cannot live according to the Sermon on the Mount. He looks at the Sermon and drools over its holiness, yet he does not know how to achieve it. He has a problem. He has a deceitful and wicked heart. Sin is the only operational force within him, keeping him chained as a prisoner. Try as he may, he cannot keep the Law. Finally he cries out, "Wretched man that I am! Who will set me free from the body of this death?" (Romans 7:24). Who will set him free from his heart that is deceitful and desperately wicked? Who will set him free from this principle of sin and death that reigns in his body?

The answer is found in Romans 8:2: "For the law of the Spirit of life in Christ Jesus has set you free from the law of sin and death."

What is God saying? Let's take a closer look. The word *law* in Romans 8:2 refers not to the Ten Commandments but to a principle. For instance, we speak of a law or a principle of gravity. Here Paul talks about two principles: the principle of the Spirit of life in Christ Jesus versus the principle of sin and death which rules in unsaved men and women. Romans 8:2, then, tells us that this principle of the Spirit of life in Christ Jesus is the principle that sets us free from the law or principle of sin and death which kept us from being righteous.

In Romans 8:3, God explains how He sets us free from this principle of sin and death.

> For what the Law could not do, weak as it was through the flesh, God *did:* sending His own Son in the likeness of sinful flesh and *as an offering* for sin, He condemned sin in the flesh.

Let's analyze what God is saying. The Law (the Ten Commandments, the Old Covenant) could not change us. It exemplified righteousness, but it could not make us righteous. It could not set us free from the principle of death indwelling our bodies. Why? Because the flesh refused to cooperate! It *couldn't* cooperate, weakened as it was by the life-sapping power of indwelling sin. Therefore, since the Law could not set us free from our flesh and indwelling sin, God set us free.

Are you saying, "WOW!"? Is your mouth hanging open in wonder?

I hope so! I pray the veil will come off your eyes and you'll see that if you are truly His, you are no longer a slave to sin. God, through the Spirit of life, has set you free from slavery to sin. Free from the law (the principle) of sin and of death.

How does God set us free? Romans 8:3 gives us the answer. God's Son took on our humanity and came in the likeness of sinful flesh as an offering for sin. When Jesus hung on the cross, God condemned sin in the flesh. That verb *condemned* is an aorist, active, indicative verb.

I know this sounds complicated, but I want you to grow so let me stretch you! The aorist tense is a punctilliar verb. It does not tell us when something occurred but simply that it did. It means "at one point in time." The active voice means that the subject performed the action of the verb. The indicative mood is the mood of reality. Therefore, God is saying that at one point in time He, all by Himself, condemned sin in your flesh. In other words, He deposed sin of its dominion or power to rule over you.

Do you see what this means, Beloved? Have you let the great, liberating reality of it grip your heart? If you are really a Christian, you are no longer enslaved to sin. *You have been set free from sin's dominion over you!* This, Beloved, is liberating. Let me show this to you in two separate passages.

Read John 8:34–36, and then answer the questions that follow:

Jesus answered them, "Truly, truly, I say to you, everyone who commits sin is the slave of sin. And the slave does not remain in the house forever; the son does remain forever. If therefore the Son shall make you free, you shall be free indeed."

1. According to Jesus, what makes us a slave of sin?

2. According to Jesus, how can you be set free from that slavery to sin?

This passage is talking about being set free from sin's power by believing on the Lord Jesus Christ. Until a person comes to salvation, he may desire to be good and please God, but because of the power of indwelling sin, he is unable to live the way he desires to live. First he must be set free from his slavery to sin. Only Jesus can set man free. How this is accomplished is explained in the next passage we want to consider.

Read through Romans 6:1–7 very carefully, which is printed out for you. Then do the assignment that follows. But first, let me urge you to stop right now and pray. Ask God to open the eyes of your understanding to the truths of Romans 6. Tell God you want to know truth…and that knowing it, you will order your life accordingly. If you are free from slavery to sin, then you will cease to believe "the lie," and you will live according to truth.

➤ ROMANS 6:1–7

1 What shall we say then? Are we to continue in sin that grace might increase?

2 May it never be! How shall we who died to sin still live in it?

3 Or do you not know that all of us who have been baptized into Christ Jesus have been baptized into His death?

4 Therefore we have been buried with Him through baptism into death, in order that as Christ was raised from the dead through the glory of the Father, so we too might walk in newness of life.

5 For if we have become united with *Him* in the likeness of His death, certainly we shall be also *in the likeness* of His resurrection,

6 knowing this, that our old self was crucified with *Him,* that our body of sin might be done away with, that we should no longer be slaves to sin;

7 for he who has died is freed from sin.

1. Now…please go back and read this passage again. This time, mark every use of the word *sin* by coloring it or underlining it. Then list below everything you learn about sin from these seven verses.

2. Read the passage one more time, and draw a tombstone like this over each use of the word *died* or *death*. What do you learn about those who died with Jesus? Write it out.

3. Read Romans 6:6. Do you see the word *that,* which occurs three times in this verse? In the second and third occurrence, *that* introduces a purpose clause. A purpose clause does just what the name implies; it gives you the purpose or the reason for something. Let me help you to see what Paul is saying in this passage.

    a. What happened to the old self or old man?

    b. Looking at that which follows, what was the purpose of this happening to the old self?

    c. What happened to the body of sin according to verse 6?

    d. According to Romans 6:6, what was the purpose for doing this to the body of sin?

4. Now according to verse 7, who is freed from sin?

In this passage God is explaining that those who are in Christ Jesus have died to sin. Verse 3 tells us that those who have been baptized into Christ Jesus have been baptized into His death. The word *baptize* does not always refer to water. There is a baptism of fire, a baptism of the Holy Spirit, a baptism of water. The children of Israel were "baptized into Moses and into the cloud."

Baptize simply means "to be identified with or united with." Therefore, Romans 6:3 is saying that those who have been united with Christ Jesus have been united into His death. I have drawn you a simple diagram to show what God is saying.

Since we have been united into His death, we will be united with Him in His burial. And according to Romans 6:5, we will also be united with Him in the likeness of His resurrection.

What God wants us to understand is this. From His perspective…
> you died with Christ,
>> you were buried with Christ,
>>> and you are raised with Christ
>>>> so that you might walk in newness of life.

Salvation brings us a whole new life because of our identification with Jesus Christ. For this reason Paul writes in 2 Corinthians 5:17: "Therefore if any man is in Christ, *he is* a new creature; the old things passed away; behold, new things have come." Old things have passed because you died with Christ. New things have come because you were raised with Christ.

What makes things new? What causes old things to pass away? How can this happen? Romans 6:6 has the answer. Our *old self*, or *old man*, was crucified with Jesus so that our body of sin might be done away with, so that we should no longer be slaves to sin. "Done away with" means "rendered powerless, inoperative."

It is interesting to note that the term "old man," or "old self," appears only three places in the New Testament: Romans 6:6; Ephesians 4:22; and Colossians 3:9. In Ephesians and Colossians the Word says that the old man, or old self, has been laid aside and the new man, the new self, has been put on. This means that everything you were before you were saved has been crucified with Jesus Christ. It is dead. It has been laid aside. You are now a new creature and are able to walk in newness of life because the death of the old man set you free. You are no longer a slave to sin.

Remember John 8:36? "If therefore the Son shall make you free, you shall be free indeed." In John 8 we saw that we are set free from being a slave to sin. And that's exactly what Romans 6 is about. The old man was crucified in order that your body, which was a slave to sin, might be set free from that slavery.

Romans 6:14 summarizes it. "For sin shall not be master over you, for you are not under law, but under grace." When you receive Jesus Christ as your Savior, you become a participant in the New Covenant, the covenant of grace which gives you the indwelling Holy Spirit. You are no longer under the Law.

And because you are no longer under the Law, sin cannot be master over you. The word *master* in the Greek means "to rule over, to lord over, or to have dominion over." Romans 6:18 says, "having been freed from sin, you became slaves of righteousness."

Now let's go back to Romans 8 and wrap it up for today. Remember we saw in Romans 8 that it is the law (or the principle) of the Spirit of life in Christ Jesus that has set us free from the law (the principle) of sin and death.

Who is it that sets us free from being a slave to sin? It is the Holy Spirit, the Spirit of life in Christ Jesus. Let me repeat it again. How did God set you free? Romans 8:3 tells us. God did it by "sending His own Son in the like-ness of sinful flesh and *as an offering* for sin."

God, through Jesus, condemned sin in the flesh. That means He deposed sin from its place of dominion. He took away the power sin needed in order to reign in your mortal body by putting to death the old self.

Why did He do it? Romans 8:4 says He did it so that you might fulfill the requirement of the Law. Listen: "in order that the requirement of the Law might be fulfilled in us, who do not walk according to the flesh, but according to the Spirit."

As you read Romans 8:1–17, you will note that Paul contrasts two things: those who are in the flesh, or walk according to the flesh, and those who are in the Spirit, or walk according to the Spirit. Those who are in the flesh are people who do not have the Spirit of God dwelling in them. Romans 8:8–9 tells us, "those who are in the flesh cannot please God. How-ever, you are not in the flesh but in the Spirit, if indeed the Spirit of God dwells in you. But if anyone does not have the Spirit of Christ, he does not belong to Him."

What God is saying is that if the Holy Spirit is not in you, then you do not belong to God. You are not a Christian.

But if you are now in Christ, "you have not received a spirit of slavery." You are no longer a slave. Remember John 8:35–36 says that "the slave does not remain in the house forever; the son does remain forever. If therefore the Son shall make you free, you shall be free indeed." When Jesus came to live inside of you, He cast out (so to speak) the slave. He put to death the old man. He set you free from slavery to sin so that you need not fear. God adopted you as His own son or daughter. For this reason Romans 8:15 tells us: "For you have not received a spirit of slavery leading to fear again, but you have received a spirit of adoption as sons by which we cry out, 'Abba! Father!'"

Now let's go back to our questions about the Sermon on the Mount. The Sermon on the Mount is a lofty but unattainable lifestyle for those who are not united with Jesus Christ in His death, burial, and resurrection. It just doesn't work — even for seemingly noble, rightly motivated men like Gandhi.

Man cannot straighten out man. Only God can do that! And that's just what He does by giving us the gift of His Holy Spirit when we enter into the New Covenant of grace.

Your next question may be, "But what about my sinful and deceitful heart? What am I going to do with it?"

Here's my answer: If you have become God's child, then He has taken care of it! We'll see that tomorrow, Beloved. Until then, meditate on these truths. They are so rich, so freeing! They are worthy of pondering. We are laying hold of the true essence of genuine Christianity.

D A Y   F O U R

Is the Sermon on the Mount an impossible lifestyle?

That's the question. What's the answer?

No!

The Sermon on the Mount was the lifestyle of Jesus, and it is the lifestyle He lives out to one degree or another in every believer.

We saw yesterday that we can be set free from sin's indwelling power over us through the work of Jesus Christ in His death, burial, and resurrection.

We saw that if the Son sets us free from the slavery of sin, we will be free indeed. When we are saved, we have newness of life, because our old man (self) was crucified so that our body, as an instrument of sin, might be rendered inoperative. Therefore, we will no longer be slaves to sin. It is the Spirit who sets us free from the law of sin and death, and it is the Holy Spirit who enables us to fulfill the just requirements of the Law (Romans 8:4). In this sense, we have a righteousness that exceeds the righteousness of the scribes and Pharisees.

Today we want to look at how the New Covenant of grace takes care of the problem of our deceitful, desperately wicked heart. The Old Covenant, the Law, reigned until John the Baptist came announcing the New

Covenant. Although the Law served as a strict tutor, teaching us the rules of obedience until faith in Jesus Christ should come, the Law could never make anyone righteous! All the Law could do was show us our sin so that we might kneel before God in poverty of spirit and humbly receive the righteousness that comes by faith. This righteousness was only possible because Jesus was made sin for us so that you and I might be made the righteousness of God in Him (2 Corinthians 5:21).

Hebrews 10:1–18 is printed out for you. Please read the whole passage carefully.

➤ HEBREWS 10:1–18

1 For the Law, since it has *only* a shadow of the good things to come *and* not the very form of things, can never by the same sacrifices year by year, which they offer continually, make perfect those who draw near.

2 Otherwise, would they not have ceased to be offered, because the worshippers, having once been cleansed, would no longer have had consciousness of sins?

3 But in those *sacrifices* there is a reminder of sins year by year.

4 For it is impossible for the blood of bulls and goats to take away sins.

5 Therefore, when He comes into the world, He says,

"SACRIFICE AND OFFERING THOU HAST NOT DESIRED,

BUT A BODY THOU HAST PREPARED FOR ME;

6 IN WHOLE BURNT OFFERINGS AND *sacrifices* FOR SIN THOU

HAST TAKEN NO PLEASURE.

7 "THEN I SAID, 'BEHOLD, I HAVE COME

(IN THE ROLL OF THE BOOK IT IS WRITTEN OF ME)

TO DO THY WILL, O GOD.'"

8 After saying above, "SACRIFICES AND OFFERINGS AND WHOLE BURNT OFFERINGS AND *sacrifices* FOR SIN THOU HAST NOT DESIRED, NOT HAST THOU TAKEN PLEASURE *in them* (which are offered according to the Law),

9 then He said, "BEHOLD, I HAVE COME TO DO THY WILL." He takes away the first in order to establish the second.

¹⁰ By this will we have been sanctified through the offering of the body of Jesus Christ once for all.

¹¹ And every priest stands daily ministering and offering time after time the same sacrifices, which can never take away sins;

¹² but He, having offered one sacrifice for sins for all time, SAT DOWN AT THE RIGHT HAND OF GOD,

¹³ waiting from that time onward UNTIL HIS ENEMIES BE MADE A FOOTSTOOL FOR HIS FEET.

¹⁴ For by one offering He has perfected for all time those who are sanctified.

¹⁵ And the Holy Spirit also bears witness to us; for after saying,

¹⁶ "THIS IS THE COVENANT THAT I WILL MAKE WITH THEM
AFTER THOSE DAYS, SAYS THE LORD:
I WILL PUT MY LAWS UPON THEIR HEART,
AND UPON THEIR MIND I WILL WRITE THEM,"
He then says,

¹⁷ "AND THEIR SINS AND THEIR LAWLESS DEEDS
I WILL REMEMBER NO MORE."

¹⁸ Now where there is forgiveness of these things, there is no longer *any* offering for sin.

Now, let's give special attention to verses 1, 9–10, 14–18. Take a minute to read those verses again, and then we will proceed.

In Hebrews 10:1 we see the Law could not make men perfect. Year after year the Jews kept offering the same sacrifices for sin, and yet those who made the sacrifices were never changed. Hebrews 10:4 says, "For it is impossible for the blood of bulls and goats to take away sins." Therefore, God sent His Son Jesus into the world. When Jesus came, He said, "Behold, I have come to do Thy will." He removed the Old Covenant of the Law in order to establish the New Covenant of grace (Hebrews 10:9).

According to these verses, through the New Covenant we are sanctified once for all through the offering of the body of Jesus Christ. The Law could not sanctify us or make us perfect, but the death of Jesus Christ can. Why?

You saw it yesterday. Because the death of Jesus Christ sets us free from sin's power and dominion.

Now let's look at Hebrews 10:14–17:

For by one offering He has perfected for all time those who are sancti-fied. And the Holy Spirit also bears witness to us...saying, *"This is the covenant that I will make with them after those days, says the LORD: I will put My laws upon their heart, and upon their mind I will write them.... And their sins and their lawless deeds I will remember no more."*

The italicized portion of the passage is a quote from the Old Testament prophet Jeremiah. The writer of Hebrews uses that quote to show how Jesus Christ inaugurated the New Covenant prophesied by Jeremiah. Let's take a look at this New Covenant and see how it takes care of our sin prob-lem — as well as the problem of our deceitful and desperately wicked heart which keeps leading us into sin. My purpose in all this is to show you how the New Covenant enables you to fulfill the Law and have a righteousness which surpasses that of the scribes and Pharisees.

Jeremiah 31:31–34 is printed out for you, but if I were you, I would also turn to it in my Bible and mark the passage so you can quickly find it.

As you read the passage, mark every occurrence of the word *covenant*. I have marked every use of the word in my Bible by highlighting the word *covenant* in red and then boxing the word in yellow.

➤ JEREMIAH 31:31–34

31 "Behold, days are coming," declares the LORD, "when I will make a new covenant with the house of Israel and with the house of Judah,

32 not like the covenant which I made with their fathers in the day I took them by the hand to bring them out of the land of Egypt, My covenant which they broke, although I was a husband to them," declares the LORD.

33 "But this is the covenant which I will make with the house of Israel after those days," declares the LORD, "I will put My law within them, and on their heart I will write it; and I will be their God, and they shall be My people.

[34] "And they shall not teach again, each man his neighbor and each man his brother, saying, 'Know the LORD,' for they shall all know Me, from the least of them to the greatest of them," declares the LORD, "for I will forgive their iniquity, and their sin I will remember no more."

1. How many covenants are mentioned in this passage? List them below, and under each one put all you learn about the covenant from Jeremiah 31:31–34.

Jeremiah is promising the house of Israel (the northern kingdom) and the house of Judah (the southern kingdom) a new covenant, which will be different from the covenant God made with their fathers when He took them out of Egypt. That covenant was the Law, given at Mt. Sinai — the covenant which they said they would keep, but broke.

Now look at Jeremiah 31:33–34. In these verses God tells us what this New Covenant will do for mankind. There are four things I want you to see, so follow me carefully.

FIRST...

He says, "I will put My law within them, and on their heart I will write it." In the Old Covenant, the Law was written on tables of stone. In the New Covenant, the Law will be written on hearts of flesh. It will not be something external, but rather *internal*. Take a minute and read 2 Corinthians 3:2–9, a passage which explains and confirms what Jeremiah teaches. As you read, mark (each in its own distinctive way) every reference to the Law and to the Spirit — along with any synonyms or pronouns. For example, any reference to the New Covenant is synonymous with the ministry of the Spirit in this passage. The ministry of death is the Law; the ministry of the Spirit, the New Covenant of grace.

➤ 2 CORINTHIANS 3:2-9

2 You are our letter, written in our hearts, known and read by all men;

3 being manifested that you are a letter of Christ, cared for by us, written not with ink, but with the Spirit of the living God, not on tablets of stone, but on tablets of human hearts.

4 And such confidence we have through Christ toward God.

5 Not that we are adequate in ourselves to consider anything as *coming* from ourselves, but our adequacy is from God,

6 who also made us adequate *as* servants of a new covenant, not of the letter, but of the Spirit; for the letter kills, but the Spirit gives life.

7 But if the ministry of death, in letters engraved on stones, came with glory, so that the sons of Israel could not look intently at the face of Moses because of the glory of his face, fading *as* it was,

8 how shall the ministry of the Spirit fail to be even more with glory?

9 For if the ministry of condemnation has glory, much more does the ministry of righteousness abound in glory.

SECOND...

He says, "I will be their God and they shall be my people." The New Covenant brings a new relationship with God. It's a relationship of possession, of ownership. God becomes yours; you become His.

THIRD...

In Jeremiah 31:34, God reveals yet more truth about the New Covenant: "They shall not teach again, each man his neighbor and each man his brother, saying, 'Know the LORD,' for they shall all know Me, from the least of them to the greatest of them."

I believe God is showing us that there will be an inward knowing of Him, a witness of God's Spirit within, teaching us about Him. What you learn from the Lord will not come merely from what teachers tell you about Him, but God Himself will be your Teacher, whispering instructions, counsel, rebuke, and encouragement from deep within your own spirit. The apostle John had the same thing in mind when he wrote: "And as for you, the anointing which you received from Him abides in you, and you have no need for anyone to teach you; but as His anointing teaches you about all things..." (1 John 2:27).

In other words, you will have a resident Teacher — the Holy Spirit.

F O U R T H ...

God says He will forgive your iniquity, and your sin He will remember no more. This is what we saw quoted by the author of Hebrews in the tenth chapter when he explains the New Covenant inaugurated by our Lord Jesus Christ.

O Beloved, if you ever get hold of this, it will open up your understanding of the Christian life in a whole new way!

Now, let's look at one last passage in Jeremiah that deals with the New Covenant. Read Jeremiah 32:38–40. As you read, mark the word *covenant* and notice what God is going to do.

> "And they shall be My people, and I will be their God; and I will give them one heart and one way, that they may fear Me always, for their own good, and for *the good of* their children after them. And I will make an everlasting covenant with them that I will not turn away from them, to do them good; and I will put the fear of Me in their hearts so that they will not turn away from Me."

Verse 38 reiterates God's promise in Jeremiah 31 — "They shall be My people, and I will be their God." In verse 39, He gives you even more insight into this New Covenant. He tells the people of Israel that He will give them one heart and one way so that they will fear Him always — for their good and for the good of their children who will come after them.

In other words, your life will be an example to your children as they see your reverence for God. This is a prophetic passage regarding the future of Israel (Israel and Judah) and their land where He will faithfully plant them. Yet, in reading this, I also see the benefits of the New Covenant in my life, because Israel's rejection of Jesus Christ and the New Covenant He brought has been my salvation.

In Jeremiah 32:40, God tells them this is an everlasting covenant. It will never end! God promises that He will never turn away from them, never stop doing them good. What an awesome promise! It reminds me of Hebrews 13:5 where God promises that He will never leave us or forsake us.

O Beloved, have you ever been afraid that you might walk away from God? That at some dark point in your life you might turn away from Him? I understand. I used to be bothered by those fears, too. But then I read Jeremiah 32:40, and my eyes were opened to God's wonderful keeping power. In the New Covenant, God promises us that He will put the fear of Him in our hearts so that we will not turn away! Praise the Lord!

This reminds me of what Paul wrote to Timothy in 2 Timothy 1:12. Paul told his young friend how convinced he was of God's ability to guard and keep what the apostle had entrusted to Him. It also calls to mind John's sober words in 1 John 2:19: "They went out from us, but they were not *really* of us; for if they had been of us, they would have remained with us; but *they went out,* in order that it might be shown that they all are not of us."

God writes His laws on your very heart. Isn't that wonderful? As a result, you have a deep inner knowledge and awareness of what pleases God and what displeases Him.

Are you ready to call it a day? I am. There's much to meditate on. Ask God to open the eyes of your understanding. How I pray you are growing, Precious One, and that I am explaining this to you in the clearest way possible. Your faces are ever before me. I so long to be one who accurately handles the Word of God. I never stop thinking about my great accountability before God as a teacher of His Word. So check me out carefully! Do your homework. Study diligently. I don't want you to believe something just because you hear it from a teacher. You are responsible to search it out in the Word for yourself.

And don't forget…the Teacher Himself dwells within you.

DAY FIVE

Finally, in this last day of study, we are going to look at a few more verses to find out how God takes care of man's deceitful and desperately wicked heart!

I want to begin by looking at Ezekiel 36:26–27 — two very significant verses. Here is God's promise of a new heart, once again prophesied to Israel but applicable to us as you will see.

"Moreover, I will give you a new heart and put a new spirit within you; and I will remove the heart of stone from your flesh and give you a heart of flesh. And I will put My Spirit within you and cause you to walk in My statutes, and you will be careful to observe My ordinances."

Ezekiel calls it "a new heart," "a heart of flesh," while in Romans 2:29 Paul calls it a "circumcised heart." Circumcision is a cutting away of the old in order to reveal the new. In Romans 2:29 we see that this circumcision is by the Spirit, and not by the letter. In other words, God is saying that heart circumcision comes through the New Covenant and not through keeping the Law. (When Paul refers to "the letter," he is speaking of the Law.)

In Ezekiel 36:26 you also see the promise of a new Spirit within. Think with me for a moment. . . . Where do the beatitudes begin? They begin with poverty of spirit. They begin with the overwhelming realization before God that you are spiritually bankrupt and utterly destitute. You are "poor in spirit" when you realize there is no way you can satisfy the holiness of God because you are devoid of the Spirit of God. But when you come to Him in your poverty of spirit (the deepest form of repentance), then God gives you the kingdom of heaven by giving you the Holy Spirit. The Spirit is not only your guarantee of redemption, He is the very means of living righteously so you can enter God's kingdom.

Listen again to what Ezekiel 36:27 says: "And I will put My Spirit within you and cause you to walk in My statutes, and you will be careful to observe My ordinances."

Here is the promise of God's indwelling Holy Spirit, the Enabler who gives us the power to keep God's laws and walk in obedience to His commandments. Here is the promise of the Spirit of life in Christ Jesus, the One who sets you free from the law of sin and death (Romans 8:2), the One who gives you a new heart!

O Beloved, by now I'm sure you have seen how impossible it is for us to fulfill the Law apart from the Spirit of God dwelling within. That is why Gandhi and others could not live out the whole Sermon on the Mount. Gandhi could turn the other cheek and go the extra mile. But he could not live it all because he did not see his own poverty of spirit and choose to walk under the lordship of Jesus Christ.

Please don't think that I am judging. It's simply that Gandhi himself never claimed to think of Jesus as anyone other than "a great man." To Gandhi, as to others, the Sermon on the Mount was simply a code of ethics, an ideal to strive for. They failed to see that it is an impossible lifestyle for those who do not have a new heart and God's Spirit living within. They all missed the first beatitude, which alone gives men the kingdom of heaven. When we bow before Him in our deep poverty of spirit, receiving His gift of salvation, He gives us His very own Spirit who *enables* us to walk in His ways.

This is what Ephesians 1:13 means when it says, "After listening to the message of truth, the gospel of your salvation — having also believed, you were sealed in Him with the Holy Spirit of promise."

Now let's put all we have learned this week into the context of Matthew 5:17–20. In verse 17 Jesus says, "Do not think that I came to abolish the Law or the Prophets; I did not come to abolish, but to fulfill." It was important that the Jews understand Jesus' relationship to the Law and the Prophets. The term "the Law and the Prophets" is a summation of all the Old Testament. Jesus was the fulfillment of the Old Testament. He was the seed of the woman in Genesis 3:15, and the seed of Abraham in Genesis 15:5–6 and Galatians 3:16. He was the personification of the righteousness of the Law who would become the curse of the Law, for "cursed is everyone who hangs on a tree" (Galatians 3:13). His dying on the very same day that the Passover lamb was sacrificed demonstrated to all who would believe that He was the Lamb of God, who would take away the sins of the world. He was the Child whom the virgin would bear as prophesied in Isaiah 7:14. His name would be called Immanuel, "God with us." He was the Child who was to be born, the Son who was to be given, the One whose name would be called Wonderful Counselor, Mighty God, Eternal Father, Prince of Peace (see Isaiah 9:6). He was the One whose bones would not be broken, who would cry out, "My God, my God, why hast Thou forsaken me?" (Psalm 22:1).

According to Zechariah 12:10, He would be the One whom the Jews would pierce and whom they would someday look upon and mourn because they did not know the day of their visitation. According to Malachi 3:1, He was the Messenger of the covenant who would come suddenly to the temple. Jesus was the fulfillment of all that the Law and the Prophets pointed to. Not one jot or tittle would pass away from the Law until He had accomplished it all. "Forever, O LORD, Thy word is settled in heaven" (Psalm 119:89).

This is why Jesus goes on to say in His Sermon on the Mount, "Whoever then annuls one of the least of these commandments, and so teaches others, shall be called least in the kingdom of heaven; but whoever keeps and teaches *them,* he shall be called great in the kingdom of heaven" (Matthew 5:19).

God's Word is not to be tampered with. The commandments are not to be annulled. Jesus came to fulfill the Law, and that is what you and I are to do also.

"But, Kay," you say, "I thought that we were now under grace, no longer under the Law!"

That's right, Beloved. But the grace we are under does not make us lawless. Grace fulfills the Law. Grace calls us to a righteousness surpassing that of the scribes and Pharisees, a righteousness that is absolutely essential if we are to enter the kingdom of heaven (Matthew 5:20). According to Romans 8:4, this is why the Holy Spirit is given to us: "in order that the requirement of the Law might be fulfilled in us, who do not walk according to the flesh, but according to the Spirit."

In Matthew 5:19 we see that if we are to be great in the kingdom of heaven, we must first keep and then teach God's commandments. Note which comes first — the keeping! And all of this is possible because God has given us His Holy Spirit.

Man cannot straighten out himself. Humanity cannot untie the knots of sin and sorrow in which it has entangled itself. But what is impossible with man is possible with God!

Have you been trying to straighten out yourself? Have you been trying to shape up? Are you totally frustrated? Do you cry out with Paul, "Wretched man that I am! Who will set me free from the body of this death?" (Romans 7:24)?

O Beloved, has God spoken to you through all this and shown you that you need a new heart? Has He shown you your need for salvation? Then come to Him in your poverty of spirit and let *Him* straighten you out. Tell Him that you repent. Tell Him you've had a change of mind, that you believe Jesus Christ is God in the flesh and He has the right to be your Lord, your Master. Tell Him you want no other master but Jesus Christ. Thank Him for sending His Son to take the penalty for your sins, that you, in turn, through believing in Him, might have His righteousness. Ask God to save you from your sin by giving you His Holy Spirit. Thank Him that He has now put to death that old man within and that He has made a brand-new you. Thank Him for freeing you from sin's dominion and enabling you to walk in newness of life as a brand-new creature in Christ Jesus. Thank Him for the gift of eternal life.

Now, record this most important day of your spiritual birth in your Bible. Welcome, Beloved, to God's forever family! How I would love to hear from you. Just put "personal re: LITBTM" on the envelope, and send it to Kay Arthur, Precept Ministries, P. O. Box 182218, Chattanooga, Tennessee, 37422. I can't wait to receive the good news of your salvation!

You've done it, my friend! You've stayed on your feet and kept hiking through the "steepest" part of this book. Now that you've climbed into the high country of God's eternal plan and purposes, the trail levels out. You will find understanding and applications to your life more readily at hand. I commend you for keeping at the task! As we journey further together, you will encounter life truths that will bring you great release — and great joy.

TORN BETWEEN TWO MASTERS

Have you ever been very, very angry — so angry you wanted someone to die? How do you control that kind of anger and rage?

Have you ever felt yourself swept along on a dark, fast current of adulterous desires? How do you control lust so that it doesn't control you?

Have you ever wondered why society demands that you take an oath and swear you are speaking the truth before you testify in court? Is it because lying has become a way of life in our culture?

In 1992 the results of America's most unusual and comprehensive poll were published in a book entitled *The Day America Told the Truth* by James Patterson. The statistics in the book alone were horrifying. But beyond those, the content becomes pornographic in places as Americans from all walks of life let their anonymous hair down and told pollsters what was *really* on their minds and in their hearts.

On "the day America told the truth," we got a glimpse into the "heart" of America — and we staggered at the news. In short, America is going to hell. Why? Because the people's righteousness does not begin to surpass the righteousness of the scribes and Pharisees of Jesus' day. As a matter of fact, we wouldn't even show up on the same graph with the scribes and Pharisees. And the Lord Jesus assured us that unless our righteousness actually *exceeded* that of the scribes and Pharisees, we would never see the kingdom of heaven.

President Ronald Reagan once spoke about America being "a city on a hill" in a dark world. But we are far from that. Even many who call themselves "Christian" in our country have failed in their dual functions of salt and light. Their testimonies no longer stop the spread of corruption; their lifestyles no longer dispel the darkness so men can see their good works and glorify their Father in heaven.

How about you, my friend? Are you an "upholder" of the commandments of God? Do you order your life according to the dictates of the Ten Commandments — the statutes of life? Or do you merely quote them?

Jesus was concerned for His disciples. He didn't want them deceived. He didn't want them lured into a false security that would land them in the eternal Lake of Fire. He wanted them to understand the narrowness of the way that leads to life, the gravity of not just hearing what He said but living accordingly. It was with these concerns on His heart that He preached the Sermon on the Mount.

As we begin our study of the remainder of Matthew 5, in particular verses 21–48, it would be profitable for you to read this portion in the back of your book and mark in two distinctive colors or symbols the following phrases:

1. "You have heard" or "You have heard that it was said" or "And it was said"

2. "But I say to you"

Once you do this, it would also be good to mark your Bible in the same way. As a matter of fact, I would urge you to consider using the *International Inductive Study Bible* in the version of your choice. Because it has wide, ample margins (in addition to unique resources to help you study inductively), I would suggest you write the notes you want to keep in the margins. In this way you will have Bible and notebook combined under one cover, and you will find yourself better prepared for the opportunities the Lord gives you to share truth one on one, or in a group setting.

As you read and meditate on the Sermon on the Mount, it becomes obvious that Christianity is not a religion — merely adhering to an external set of rules. It is, rather, *hungering and thirsting for righteousness* — a righteousness that is an inside-out reality. It is a righteousness of the heart.

In Matthew 5:21–48, Jesus gives his hearers six examples of how their righteousness is to exceed the righteousness of the scribes and Pharisees. He deals with murder (21–26), adultery (27–32), divorce (31–32), vows (33–37), and revenge (38–42). Then He talks about relationships and loving our enemies (43–48).

As we study, it is important for us to realize that Jesus is not giving his listeners teaching that conflicts with the Law of Moses. This He could not do, because Jesus did not come to abolish the Law but to fulfill it. Neither is He giving "another law." That would violate His own words in Matthew 5:19: "Whoever then annuls one of the least of these commandments, and so teaches others, shall be called least in the kingdom of heaven; but whoever keeps and teaches *them,* he shall be called great in the kingdom of heaven."

As you read Matthew 5, it is crucial that you understand what Jesus is doing. He is not in any way altering the Law or diminishing it; rather He is showing His hearers *the true intent of the Law.* Why? Because the scribes and Pharisees had seated themselves in the chair of Moses. In doing so they required rigid observance of 365 prohibitions and 250 commandments. In all their prohibitions and additional commandments, they had tied heavy, unbearable loads on the people's shoulders and said, "This is the righteousness that God requires. Keep these laws and you will be pleasing to Him."

This exacting, external, heavy-handed kind of "righteousness," however, dealt only with the outward appearance. It left men's and women's hearts unchanged. For this reason, Jesus had to show them the true heart of the Law.

Could this possibly be the problem today among those who go to church, profess to know God, throw a cloak of rationalization over their ungodly behavior, and still claim the name of "Christian"? Let's see how we measure up. One by one, look at the examples Jesus gave. Read Matthew 5:21–26, and then write your answers.

I'm going to print out the passage for you right here so you can easily keep it before you as you answer these questions.

➤ MATTHEW 5:21–26

21 "You have heard that the ancients were told, 'YOU SHALL NOT COM-MIT MURDER' and 'Whoever commits murder shall be liable to the court.'

22 "But I say to you that everyone who is angry with his brother shall be guilty before the court; and whoever shall say to his brother, 'Raca,' shall be guilty before the supreme court; and whoever shall say, 'You fool,' shall be guilty *enough to go* into the fiery hell.

23 "If therefore you are presenting your offering at the altar, and there remember that your brother has something against you,

24 leave your offering there before the altar, and go your way; first be reconciled to your brother, and then come and present your offering.

25 "Make friends quickly with your opponent at law while you are with him on the way, in order that your opponent may not deliver you to the judge, and the judge to the officer, and you be thrown into prison.

26 "Truly I say to you, you shall not come out of there, until you have paid up the last cent."

1. What had they heard?

2. How does Jesus respond? Does He contradict what they had heard? What in essence does Jesus say? Summarize it in your own words.

3. According to Matthew 5:22, man will be held accountable for three other things. These are denoted by the words *everyone* and *whoever*. What are they?

4. What are Jesus' instructions in verses 23–24?

5. What are Jesus' instructions in verses 25–26?

Now let's take apart these six verses point by point.

God's concern for the sanctity of life came long before Moses received the commandment, "You shall not murder" (Exodus 20:13). From the Garden of Eden man has been considered his brother's keeper. When an angry Cain rose up and killed Abel, God did not let his crime go unpunished. Life matters to God.

After the ark rested upon the mountains of Ararat, God made the sanctity of human life very clear to Noah by instituting capital punishment.

"And surely I will require your lifeblood; from every beast I will require it. And from *every* man, from every man's brother I will require the life of man. Whoever sheds man's blood, by man his blood shall be shed, for in the image of God He made man." (Genesis 9:5–6)

Murder is a hideous crime because it contradicts the value God has placed upon human life. Marred or not, man was made in the image of God. To murder a man or woman is to destroy what God created, and only God has the right of life and death.

At this point you may say, "Kay, that's the very reason why I am *against* capital punishment. Who are we to play God and take another person's life?"

And I would have to ask in return, "Who are we to break God's Law?"

The King James Version translates Exodus 20:13, "Thou shalt not kill," but the Hebrew word literally means "to murder intentionally." Hence, the New American Standard Bible renders it, "You shall not murder." This is God's command. It is very plain. Murder is a sin. That sin must be punished. How? "Whoever sheds man's blood, by man his blood shall be shed" (Genesis 9:6).

But what if someone did not intentionally kill a man? What if it was an accident? God made provision for this in Exodus 21:12–14.

"He who strikes a man so that he dies shall surely be put to death. But if he did not lie in wait *for him,* but God let *him* fall into his hand, then I will appoint you a place to which he may flee. If, however, a man acts presumptuously toward his neighbor, so as to kill him craftily, you are to take him *even* from My altar, that he may die."

God had the Israelites establish three cities of refuge. When a man killed another man unintentionally, he could flee to one of the cities of refuge and live there (Deuteronomy 19:1–4). However, if a man had murdered another and then ran to a city of refuge, the elders of that city could take him out and deliver him to the avenger of blood that he might die. They were not to take pity upon him but were to purge the blood of the innocent from Israel so that it might go well with the nation (Deuteronomy 19:11–13).

I am giving you these extra scriptures so that you might have a biblical view of capital punishment and so that you might understand what Jesus is saying about anger and the sanctity of life.

Look at Matthew 5:22. We have seen that murder was wrong and was to be judged in a court where the just penalty would be carried out. However, Jesus goes on to tell us that everyone who is angry with his brother should be guilty before the court. Anyone who calls his brother "Raca" should be guilty before the supreme court, the Sanhedrin. And everyone who would refer to a brother as a fool would be guilty enough to go to Gehenna, the Lake of Fire.

What is Jesus trying to show us? I think He wants us to see the value of a person. Murder, like all other sins, has its beginning in a man's heart. Matthew 15:19 says, "For out of the heart come evil thoughts, murders, adulteries, fornications, thefts, false witness, slanders. These are the things which defile the man." You can murder a man in your heart without ever killing him physically. Murder begins with anger.

There is a righteous anger and there is an unrighteous anger. We see righteous anger demonstrated in the life of Jesus Christ when He overturned the tables of the moneychangers in the temple. We see this righteous anger in God when He wanted Moses to get out of His way so He could destroy the nation of Israel.

Ephesians 4:26 says, "BE ANGRY AND *yet* DO NOT SIN; do not let the sun go down on your anger." The word *angry* in Ephesians 4:26 is the same word as used in Matthew 5:22. Obviously, when Paul writes "be angry, and do not sin," that type of anger cannot be sin in God's eyes. Yet when Jesus uses that very same word to say that everyone who is angry with his brother shall be guilty before the court, He is speaking about a wrong and sinful kind of anger.

What's the difference? What makes it wrong? In the context of Scripture, we see that it is wrong because it is directed toward the sinner rather than the sin. It is an anger that, if unchecked, could lead to murder. Therefore, if you are going to be righteous before God, you cannot permit this kind of anger in your heart. It is not wrong for you to become indignant over sin, but it is wrong for you to have an anger within your heart that would destroy a man who is made in God's image. This is why saying *Raca* is so bad.

Raca is an Aramaic word for empty-headed, or good-for-nothing. How can I use such a term to describe a man or woman made in God's image, created to glorify Him? Who am I to ascribe that kind of label to one given life by the Creator, formed by the Lord in the secret place of the womb? Who am I, another human being, to sit in the seat of God and tell another person that he or she is not worth anything? Isn't that a form of murder — saying his life has no value, no purpose, that there is no reason for his existence?

Jesus also tells us we are not to say to another, "you fool."

To call a man a fool is to disdain the fact that God has given him life. The word *fool* is *moros*. From the context of Matthew 5:22, we can see that the word *fool* is a degree worse than *Raca*. W. E. Vine says, "*[Raca]* scorns a man's mind and calls him stupid; *moros* scorns his heart and character; hence the Lord's more severe condemnation." *Fool* means morally worthless.

If Matthew 5:48 summarizes everything that precedes it, and we are to be perfect even as our heavenly Father is perfect, *then we must view others in the same way that God does.* We must value every person.

How far does this respect for life go? It goes so far that if you know your brother has something against you, you are *immediately* to seek reconciliation. That is how important relationships are to God. Just before Jesus went to Calvary, He prayed to the Father that we might be one even as He and His Father are one (John 17:20–21). God does not want a schism in the body. Our gifts and our prayers mean nothing to Him if we are not going to walk in peace with our brothers.

Can you see that it is not the letter of the Law God is interested in, but the *spirit* of the Law? External conformity is not enough. Internal righteousness is what He requires. Remember the beatitude, "Blessed are the pure in heart"?

We have seen truth, and now, my friend, we must apply it.

What is your heart's attitude toward other individuals as you interact in the marketplace, as you move in the business world, as you sit behind the desk as a teacher, as you fulfill the role of a parent, as you live with your mate? How does your heart feel toward those with whom you come into contact? Do you respect them as created by God in His image, distorted as it may be? Do you value the sanctity of their lives…or do you despise God's creation? What is in your heart?

Take a few minutes to take stock of your attitudes toward others. Ask God to search you and see if there is any wicked way in you that you might confess it, turn from it, and embrace a righteousness that is not of the letter but is of the spirit.

D A Y   T W O

"What's wrong with pornography? After all, all you're doing is *looking!* What man is there that doesn't have some stashed somewhere — or at least doesn't want to take a little peek at it…maybe on television, late at night after the family has gone to bed?"

"What's wrong with a woman fantasizing about being with men other than her husband — as long as she doesn't pursue it? After all, no one's going to know…and besides, it helps her tolerate the dullness of her marriage bed."

"My husband likes to rent those explicit movies…he says it improves our sexual relationship. We watch them in the privacy of our home after the kids are in bed. I feel dirty, but…he says there's nothing wrong with it."

From murder, Jesus moves to adultery. Could the above illustrations be the reason why?

A person's sexual conduct serves as a barometer of his or her relationship with God. This comes out so clearly in Romans 1, where Paul speaks about what happens when people deliberately reject the truth of God. God gives them up to the lusts of their hearts, to impurity, to the dishonoring of their bodies. From there it's a downhill slide into lesbianism and homosexuality and eventually to a reprobate mind which knows no moral absolutes and which delights in others who live the same kind of lifestyle.

At the bottom of the hill there's a chasm that drops off into destruction and hell. Where are we as a nation? Near the bottom of the hill? Over the edge into the chasm? Or are we in denial?

Recently I spoke with a young man who was grieved over his mother's actions. My heart hurt as he told me the classic story that is repeated endlessly in homes across America. His mother had left his dad for another man. That man had left his wife, entangling two families in the web of adultery.

The action itself was bad enough. But the mother's response made it even worse.

"Mom says I'm living under legalism when I tell her that she is not doing right," the grieving young man told me. "She says that she's 'under grace' and not to worry about her."

Does grace allow us habitually to commit physical or mental adultery? Where does adultery really begin?

Let's see what Jesus has to say about the subject. Read Matthew 5:27–32, which is printed out for you. As you read, mark in distinctive ways the following words: *adultery, lust, heart,* and *hell.*

➤ MATTHEW 5:27-32

27 "You have heard that it was said, 'YOU SHALL NOT COMMIT ADULTERY';

28 but I say to you, that everyone who looks on a woman to lust for her has committed adultery with her already in his heart.

29 "And if your right eye makes you stumble, tear it out, and throw it from you; for it is better for you that one of the parts of your body perish, than for your whole body to be thrown into hell.

30 "And if your right hand makes you stumble, cut it off, and throw it from you; for it is better for you that one of the parts of your body perish, than for your whole body to go into hell.

31 "And it was said, 'WHOEVER SENDS HIS WIFE AWAY, LET HIM GIVE HER A CERTIFICATE OF DIVORCE';

32 but I say to you that everyone who divorces his wife, except for *the* cause of unchastity, makes her commit adultery; and whoever marries a divorced woman commits adultery."

Now, list below what constitutes adultery according to the Lord Jesus Christ.

According to this passage, how important is it that a person controls his or her lust, and why?

What is Jesus' recommendation for those having a problem with lust, and why?

What do you believe Jesus means when He says pluck out your eye, cut off your hand?

Now that you have observed the text, let's talk about it. I sincerely wish we could do it in person so we'd make sure we really understood one another. For now, however, we'll have to make do with the printed page!

If you shared Jesus' words, "Everyone who looks on a woman to lust for her has committed adultery with her already in his heart" (Matthew 5:28) with someone, what might be that person's response? Some would retort, "You mean to tell me that if I just have a dirty thought come into my mind, a thought about sex, I've committed adultery?"

It may sound like Jesus is saying that in this text, but He isn't. The verb *look* is in the present tense in the Greek, implying a continuous or habitual action. Jesus is saying if you *keep on looking* at a woman or a man, to lust after that woman or man, you have committed adultery with that person in your heart. Remember what we saw yesterday in Matthew 15:18–19? It might help us to look at the verses again:

> "But the things that proceed out of the mouth come from the heart, and those defile the man. For out of the heart come evil thoughts, murders, adulteries, fornications, thefts, false witness, slanders."

"For out of the heart come...adulteries"! Adultery begins a long time before you ever get into bed with another person.

It begins with a look that is not brought under control.

It begins with a thought that is not turned away but entertained.

Was Jesus' evaluation of adultery something new? Oh, no! Job understood it well. Turn to Job 31:1–12. We will print it out, but first I want you to see it in your own Bible so that you can mark it and remember where it is. As a matter of fact, at the top of that page in your Bible you might write "a covenant with my eyes." As you read, you might want to mark the words *iniquity* and *lustful crime,* as well as the word *heart* (just draw a red heart over it — or maybe it should be black!).

➤ J O B   3 1 : 1 – 1 2

1 "I have made a covenant with my eyes;

How then could I gaze at a virgin?

2 "And what is the portion of God from above

Or the heritage of the Almighty from on high?

3 "Is it not calamity to the unjust,

And disaster to those who work iniquity?

4 "Does He not see my ways,

And number all my steps?

5 "If I have walked with falsehood,

And my foot has hastened after deceit,

6 Let Him weigh me with accurate scales,

And let God know my integrity.

7 "If my step has turned from the way,

Or my heart followed my eyes,

Or if any spot has stuck to my hands,

8 Let me sow and another eat,

And let my crops be uprooted.

9 "If my heart has been enticed by a woman,

Or I have lurked at my neighbor's doorway,

10 May my wife grind for another,

And let others kneel down over her.

11 "For that would be a lustful crime;

Moreover, it would be an iniquity *punishable*

by judges.

12 "For it would be fire that consumes to

Abaddon,

And would uproot all my increase."

According to this passage, what is the danger with the eyes? Can you relate?

What is the punishment mentioned in this passage for allowing your heart to follow your eyes?

(You know, I see this happen so often with men. They have an affair, their heart becomes involved, and they find it hard to say no or walk away from the affair. But they never stop to think of what they are doing to the wife of their youth, the mother of their children, and the children themselves. Then one day they wake up, cold reality sets in...and it's too late. They lie in a bed they made and miss the peaceful fruit of obedience — the holidays, the children, the grandchildren, and all the events which were to be the succulent fruit of fidelity and integrity. They've "uprooted all their increase" — and they are left a dried-up, disconnected branch.)

Job had a godly fear that held his passions in check. He knew God saw his way and numbered all his steps. Fully aware of the weaknesses of his flesh, of the ability of a man's heart to be enticed by a woman, Job determined to flee lust by making a covenant with his eyes. He would not permit them to gaze on what would entice him and consume his righteousness. No pornography for Job! No late-night television for this godly man!

Remember the young man's mother who called her son "legalistic" when he held her accountable for her adultery? Her condition is obvious, isn't it? The young man's mother has been enticed by sin. She lurked at her neighbor's doorway. She committed a lustful crime that would consume her and uproot and destroy the blessing of life that God had intended for her.

She's counting on grace, but according to Jude she is an ungodly person who has turned the grace of our God into licentiousness. She has denied her Master and Lord, Jesus Christ (Jude 4).

Is He in fact her Master and Lord, or could that simply be what she has *called* Jesus? Remember, Beloved, the Sermon on the Mount ends with Jesus telling those who call Him "Lord, Lord" to depart from Him because they are practicing lawlessness; they are not doing the will of the Father.

How serious is adultery? It is so serious it can take you to hell. In Galatians 5:19–21 Paul writes, "Now the deeds of the flesh are evident, which are: immorality, impurity, sensuality, idolatry, sorcery, enmities, strife, jealousy, outbursts of anger, disputes, dissensions, factions, envyings, drunkenness, carousing, and things like these, of which I forewarn you just as I have forewarned you that those who practice such things shall not inherit the kingdom of God."

The person who practices adultery will not inherit the kingdom of God. He or she will spend eternity in hell. As you read, pay close attention. I did not say a single act of adultery would keep a person from entering the kingdom of heaven. That is not what God is saying. He is saying that if adultery is *the practice of your life*, then you will not enter the kingdom of heaven. The verb that is translated *practice* in Galatians 5:21 is in the present tense; it is a habitual or continuous action in a person's life.

How serious is this matter of adultery? America certainly needs to know because we are a nation of adulterers. Immorality abounds on every hand. Sex permeates almost every aspect of our culture. Even the rough and tumble sport of football is not immune. Scantily clothed cheerleaders parade their wares for all to see. Where are a man's eyes safe? Or a woman's? Adultery is awakened by what the eye sees or what the hand touches. For this reason, Jesus tells us, "If your right eye makes you stumble, tear it out, and throw it from you.... if your right hand makes you stumble, cut it off, and throw it from you; for it is better for you that one of the parts of your body perish, than for your whole body to go into hell" (Matthew 5:29–30).

What is God advocating? Is Jesus telling you to literally pull out your eye? To literally cut off your hand? I don't believe so. I think He is using a hyperbole to make his point. Jesus is saying that adultery is a sin that can take you to hell. Therefore, get rid of anything that would cause you to commit adultery. Bring it under control. If you don't, it will destroy you!

> Do not be deceived; neither fornicators, nor idolaters, nor adulterers, nor effeminate, nor homosexuals, nor thieves, nor *the* covetous, nor drunkards, nor revilers, nor swindlers, shall inherit the kingdom of God. (1 Corinthians 6:9–10)

If you are not going to inherit the kingdom of God, then your whole body will be thrown into hell: the Lake of Fire, where the worm dies not and the fire is not quenched. Therefore, whatever you have to do to keep yourself from committing adultery, do it. Do not put yourself in a position of vulnerability. The spirit is willing but the flesh is weak.

Is it any wonder that our teens are immoral? Look at their examples. Look at the hours they spend in front of the television or at the movies. What are they seeing over and over and over again? The first two things Jesus deals with in Matthew 5: murder and adultery.

I believe if Christians don't slow their pace and discipline their time in order to be in the Word of God on a daily basis, we are going to see more and more immorality. Why? Because when we're not in the Word — reading it through consistently — we forget who our God is and what He expects and requires. We have a tendency to rationalize our humanity and forget His holiness.

We lose our perspective of eternity and become ensnared in the temporal. We lose that burning, overriding passion fueled by truth which brings the passions of our flesh into subjection. We lose the heart-desire to be holy, to please God, to be perfect even as our heavenly Father is perfect. We lose that driving inner hunger for righteousness which comes in those quiet moments of meditation as we sit at the feet of the Most High God in prayer and adoration.

Solomon eloquently warned of this tendency of ours. (As it turned out, he should have listened to his own godly counsel!)

➤ PROVERBS 4:20–27

My son, give attention to my words;
Incline your ear to my sayings.
Do not let them depart from your sight;
Keep them in the midst of your heart.
For they are life to those who find them,
And health to all their whole body.
Watch over your heart with all diligence,
For from it *flow* the springs of life.
Put away from you a deceitful mouth,
And put devious lips far from you.
Let your eyes look directly ahead,
And let your gaze be fixed straight in front of you.
Watch the path of your feet,
And all your ways will be established.
Do not turn to the right nor to the left;
Turn your foot from evil.

➤ PROVERBS 5:15, 18–23

Drink water from your own cistern,
And fresh water from your own well....
Let your fountain be blessed,
And rejoice in the wife of your youth.
As a loving hind and a graceful doe,
Let her breasts satisfy you at all times;
Be exhilarated always with her love.
For why should you, my son, be exhilarated with an adulteress,
And embrace the bosom of a foreigner?
For the ways of a man are before the eyes of the LORD,
And He watches all his paths.

His own iniquities will capture the wicked,
And he will be held with the cords of his sin.
He will die for lack of instruction,
And in the greatness of his folly he will go astray.

D A Y   T H R E E

The Jews knew that they were not to commit adultery. It was a clear violation of God's Law. So when they got tired of their wives, they simply wrote
a bill of divorce, divorcing them for any reason whatsoever.

How did they justify such actions? It was through a perverse twisting of
Deuteronomy 24:1–4. They distorted what God said in order to justify
their actions and the hardness of their hearts. Instead of seeing Deuteronomy 24:1–4 as a protection for the woman abandoned by her husband,
they used it as a proof-text for their selfishness and sin! If anything about
their wives displeased them, they would accuse them of "uncleanness."
Then, after pronouncing, "I divorce you, I divorce you, I divorce you," it
was done! The bill of divorcement could be written.

In the Sermon on the Mount, after discussing adultery, Jesus addressed
that painful issue of divorce.

> "And it was said, 'WHOEVER SENDS HIS WIFE AWAY, LET HIM GIVE
> HER A CERTIFICATE OF DIVORCE'; but I say to you that everyone who
> divorces his wife, except for *the* cause of unchastity, makes her commit
> adultery; and whoever marries a divorced woman commits adultery."
> (Matthew 5:31–32)

God hates divorce. The sin of the Jews in divorcing their wives was not
just a New Testament problem. It was a situation God addressed after the
nation had returned to the land following their seventy years in captivity. In
the book of Malachi, God is very upset with the priests. Here is what the
text shows us:

> "You cover the altar of the LORD with tears, with weeping and with
> groaning, because He no longer regards the offering or accepts *it with*

favor from your hand. Yet you say, 'For what reason?' Because the LORD has been a witness between you and the wife of your youth, against whom you have dealt treacherously, though she is your companion and wife by covenant. But not one has done so who has a remnant of the Spirit. And what did *that* one *do* while he was seeking a godly offspring? Take heed then, to your spirit, and let no one deal treacherously against the wife of your youth. For I hate divorce," says the LORD, the God of Israel, "and him who covers his garment with wrong." (Malachi 2:13–16)

God was far from them because He hates divorce. It mars His earthly example of the heavenly union of Christ to His bride, of His commitment to the nation of Israel, who is referred to as God's wife.

How I pray, Beloved, that you will see that "the body is not for immorality, but for the Lord; and the Lord is for the body.... Flee immorality. Every *other* sin that a man commits is outside the body, but the immoral man sins against his own body" (1 Corinthians 6:13, 18).

Sexual immorality leaves an awful, ugly scar.

It is a scar that deeply mars the beauty of God's creation.

It is a scar I myself have borne.

Is it any wonder, then, that after I came to know Jesus Christ, 1 Corinthians 6:19–20 became such a precious passage of Scripture to me?

Do you not know that your body is a temple of the Holy Spirit who is in you, whom you have from God, and that you are not your own? For you have been bought with a price: therefore glorify God in your body.

Have you ever thought of God's cure for AIDS? It's called preventive medicine! If we had obeyed God...if we would obey God...AIDS would not be at epidemic proportions. Yet as it stands now, the deadly disease may soon become the number one cause of death among teenagers.

O Beloved, make a covenant with your eyes that you will not look upon another with lust. Decide in advance not to commit adultery — even in your secret thoughts. Honor that marriage covenant; honor it out of obedience to God. I'd like to move on to another point here...but in all conscience, I really can't. Do you know why? It's because I feel in my spirit that some who are reading this are *at this very moment* caught in a lust, in a desire, in a dream!

It's wrong and you know it. It's sin and you know it. The Bible puts it very clearly. "Fornicators and adulterers God will judge" (Hebrews 13:4). I know you think you can't bear to do without the one you want, that if you can't have that person, life is not worth living.

You're wrong. You *will* survive. In fact, life will not be worth living if you transgress God's holy commandments! If you are a Christian, the Holy Spirit is your Resource — constantly available. Walk by the Spirit, and you will not fulfill the lust of the flesh. Make the phone call. Do not go to see him or her in person. Tell this individual that the relationship is over and there is nothing more to say or discuss. Ask his or her forgiveness, and say you have chosen to obey your Master. Then get on your knees and ask God to break your heart as you have broken His so that you will abhor your sin and flee.

Flee, Beloved, flee!

D A Y   F O U R

I had just finished teaching at one of our annual Teen Conferences on Ephesians 4:17–5:18 — a passage which deals with some tough issues that scratch teens right where they itch.

One of the things we discussed was cheating, a common problem with teens today, even in Christian high schools. Among the kids who hung around after the conference to talk, share, and pray was one very precious young lady.

"Kay," she said, "I don't do the other things you mentioned. I really walk pretty straight except for one thing. I cheat. Kay, what do I do? God says that we are to expose the deeds of darkness, but how can I expose them when I myself cheat? I'm going to stop cheating — but what do I say to my teachers? What do I say to the kids I've helped cheat?"

It's difficult to describe the love I felt welling up in my heart for this young woman. I know it was the love of the Lord. Our God loves integrity.

Here was a young woman who wanted to be honest before God and man. I can't wait to get her letter to hear how it goes when she speaks to teacher after teacher, confesses her sin, and offers to take the penalty or make restitution. I can't wait to hear what happens as she stands before her classmates and asks their forgiveness for marring the image of Jesus Christ by cheating.

God is concerned with our integrity, with the honesty of the words of our mouths. Our yeses are to be yes and our noes are to be no. What we say we are to mean. Our pledges are not to be broken. Our words are not to be couched in deceit.

Jesus took His hearers back to the Old Testament law on making vows, showing them how that law had become twisted and how they had missed its true intent. Let's look closely at what He said.

Read Matthew 5:33–37, printed out for you, and then answer the questions that follow.

➤ MATTHEW 5:33–37

33 "Again, you have heard that the ancients were told, 'YOU SHALL NOT MAKE FALSE VOWS, BUT SHALL FULFILL YOUR VOWS TO THE LORD.'

34 "But I say to you, make no oath at all, either by heaven, for it is the throne of God,

35 or by the earth, for it is the footstool of His feet, or by Jerusalem, for it is THE CITY OF THE GREAT KING.

36 "Nor shall you make an oath by your head, for you cannot make one hair white or black.

37 "But let your statement be, 'Yes, yes' or 'No, no'; and anything beyond these is of evil."

1. According to Matthew 5:33, what did the Law say about making vows?

2. Matthew 5:34–36 lists four things by which they were not to swear. What are they?

3. Now, let's look at what the Old Testament taught about vows or oaths. Read the following scriptures, and next to each, write what you learn. Determine in each instance whether an oath or a vow was wrong.

a. Leviticus 19:11–12

"You shall not steal, nor deal falsely, nor lie to one another. And you shall not swear falsely by My name, so as to profane the name of your God; I am the LORD."

b. Numbers 30:1–2

Then Moses spoke to the heads of the tribes of the sons of Israel, saying, "This is the word which the LORD has commanded. If a man makes a vow to the LORD, or takes an oath to bind himself with a binding obligation, he shall not violate his word; he shall do according to all that proceeds out of his mouth."

c. Genesis 24:2–3

And Abraham said to his servant, the oldest of his household, who had charge of all that he owned, "Please place your hand under my thigh, and I will make you swear by the LORD, the God of heaven and the God of earth, that you shall not take a wife for my son from the daughters of the Canaanites, among whom I live."

d. Deuteronomy 23:21–23

"When you make a vow to the LORD your God, you shall not delay to pay it, for it would be sin in you, and the LORD your God will surely require it of you. However, if you refrain from vowing, it would not be sin in you. You shall be careful to perform what goes out from your lips, just as you have voluntarily vowed to the LORD your God, what you have promised."

Now then, let's draw some conclusions.

1. Did the Old Testament forbid vows or oaths?

2. What was the purpose of vows? In other words, why were men permitted or allowed to make oaths?

3. Summarize, in general, what you have learned from these scriptures about making oaths or vows.

It's obvious that people living under the Old Testament Law were permitted to make vows. A vow made an agreement binding. It was a man's means of saying, "I promise you that I am going to do what I said," whether he said it to God or to man. We see this in the incident of Abraham and his servant. When his servant put his hand under Abraham's thigh, he was pledging himself by all of his strength that he would fulfill the word of his master.

We could look at many more Old Testament passages on vows, but if we did, it would only confirm what we have already seen: oaths were in accordance with God's Law. They were a call or a pledge to integrity. A man who made a vow was saying, "I am sincere. I will be honest to carry out what I'm saying."

What then was Jesus teaching in the Sermon on the Mount? Was He altering God's law? Or was this a *fulfillment* of that law? Think on it and we will talk about it more tomorrow. Right now, let me ask you some questions in love.

Are you a man or woman of integrity or honesty?

Is your Christian walk honest before God?

Can others trust you...or do you cheat? Cheating can take all sorts of forms. It doesn't necessarily have to be in school when you take an exam. You can cheat the government. You can cheat on contracts. You can fail to tell the whole truth. You can pad the statistics for emphasis. You can advertise and exaggerate. You can tell "little white lies." You can save your neck by getting around your words.

You can do all these things, but then, Beloved, where is your integrity?

Isn't that the issue in our world today — integrity?

What's your contribution to the moral fiber of our nation? Can you say what Paul said in the midst of a corrupt Roman Empire?

> Be imitators of me, just as I also am of Christ.... Join in following my example, and observe those who walk according to the pattern you have in us. For many walk, of whom I often told you, and now tell you even weeping, *that they are* enemies of the cross of Christ, whose end is destruction, whose god is *their* appetite, and *whose* glory is in their shame, who set their minds on earthly things. (1 Corinthians 11:1; Philippians 3:17–19)

D A Y   F I V E

There is a great deal of similarity between the Sermon on the Mount and the Book of James.

In James 5:12 we read, "But above all, my brethren, do not swear, either by heaven or by earth or with any other oath; but let your yes be yes, and your no, no; so that you may not fall under judgment."

Both Matthew and James remind us of the need for the integrity of our lips.

Dwight Pentecost, in his book *The Sermon on the Mount* summarizes so well what Jesus is saying:

> Let your character, your reputation for honesty, your word be so obviously true and undefiled and without duplicity, that no man would think it necessary to put you under an oath because he suspects you are of deception.... Some words can have a double meaning, and some words can be interpreted in two different ways. But there is only one possible way of interpreting yes. Yes does not mean no. There is only one way you can interpret no. You can never interpret that as meaning consent. When you say yes, it means yes; when you say no, it means no. The Lord demanded that one's speech be so trustworthy that men would not have to debate what was meant and interpret what was said. They would know what was meant because he was an honest man.[1]

As I was praying recently, the Lord revealed something painful to me. He showed me that I needed to go to my video department here at Precept Ministries, gather the people as a group, and ask them to forgive me. I had fallen under their judgment and, of course, God's also. My yes had not been yes, and my no had not been no. There had been times — too many times — when I had made agreements to cut certain things for the video department, and they had arranged their schedules accordingly. Then, because of other pressures that came upon me, I sought to alter the commitment I had made. Their hearts' desire is to help me and to assist me in the ministry that God has called me to, and I so appreciate the preciousness of their hearts and attitudes. Yet, you can imagine how frustrating it is to have your schedule constantly changed!

When one of our staff from the video department was talking with me this week about scheduling, she said, "Kay, I just want our yes to be yes and our no to be no. So let's think very carefully before we rush into our scheduling." At the time I tried to justify myself, and yet when I hung up the phone, God began to speak to me. Clearly I was wrong. It is still Sunday as I write today's lesson. Tomorrow when the offices open, I *will* make a date with the video staff. You see, Beloved, above all else I want to be a godly woman. And to be a godly woman I must have integrity in every aspect of my life.

There are tears in my eyes as I share this; I mourn because I have hurt my God. I have failed to be "perfect" even as my heavenly Father is perfect. You see, His yes is yes and His no is no. It is so wonderful, isn't it? We can *trust* our Father because He stands by His Word. He will not alter the word that has gone from His lips. I want to be like Him, don't you?

May I make a suggestion? Spend the rest of today's study time in prayer. Ask your Father to show you if you are failing in any way to let your yes be yes or your no, no.

Do you keep your word to your children?

Do you keep your word to your mate?

Do you hedge?

Are you like me, in that many times you promise things you have a desire to do and yet you are not absolutely sure you can fulfill? Sometimes it seems that my heart's desires go far beyond my abilities and a twenty-four-hour day.

I am going to search my heart. Why don't you search yours? I'm going to tell God to remind me, over and over, to watch the commitments I make with my mouth. With David, I will pray:

> Set a guard, O LORD, over my mouth;
> Keep watch over the door of my lips.
> (Psalm 141:3)

WHEN YOU ARE HURT AND CHEATED

The United States of America has the highest crime rate per capita of any nation on the earth.

Why is that?

Our federal, state, and county jails are so overcrowded that men and women are convicted of felonies and then promptly released with little more than a slap on the hand. So what do most of them do? They go out to commit the same crimes all over again. Or worse. The innocent are in danger, while the criminals go free.

What are we doing wrong?

If we lived under God's judicial system — an eye for an eye, a tooth for a tooth, a life for a life — do you think we would find ourselves in the same situation? Do you think our judicial system is *better?* Are we more effective in dealing with man's injustice to man?

These are questions worth pondering, worth studying. And we will! We're going to think through these things together as we look at Jesus' teaching in the Sermon on the Mount in Matthew 5:38–42:

38 "You have heard that it was said, 'AN EYE FOR AN EYE, AND A TOOTH FOR A TOOTH.'

39 "But I say to you, do not resist him who is evil; but whoever slaps you on your right cheek, turn to him the other also.

40 "And if anyone wants to sue you, and take your shirt, let him have your coat also.

41 "And whoever shall force you to go one mile, go with him two.

42 "Give to him who asks of you, and do not turn away from him who wants to borrow from you."

Tell me something…was Jesus *changing* the Law by making statements like these? Was He saying, in essence, "What you heard was wrong"?

No. He wasn't saying that at all. As we reflect on these things, we must bear in mind that there were no printing presses until the 1400s A.D. All writing was painstakingly done on scrolls, then hand copied by scribes. The ordinary man did not have his own copy of the Word of God. The way he knew the Word was to hear it read in the synagogue. Jesus wasn't saying what they heard was wrong, nor was He changing the Law. Along with Paul, Jesus could have said, "The Law is holy, and the commandment is holy and righteous and good" (Romans 7:12). Jesus would not change it. On the contrary, He came to *fulfill* the Law.

But if He wasn't altering the Law, what was He doing when He said we are not to resist him who is evil?

Once again, Jesus is taking us to the heart of the matter. He is going to show us that righteous men and women are controlled by a much higher law.

In the next two days I hope to cover this passage in a fairly comprehensive way. And the subject matter won't always be easy to deal with. If it is hard to understand "an eye for an eye and a tooth for a tooth," it is even harder to understand turning the other cheek when someone slaps you! And if someone wants to sue you and take your shirt, what do you think about giving him your coat also? If people keep asking of you and wanting to borrow from you, are you to give them everything you have? And when people force you to go one mile, why on earth should you go with them two? Isn't one enough?

These are all legitimate questions that need legitimate answers. I pray that in the next two days you'll have God's insight so that you can know how to live in the light of Matthew 5:38–42.

First, let's look at "an eye for an eye, and a tooth for a tooth." Where did this expression come from?

Let's take a look at this law in the light of its context in Exodus 21:1, 12–31.

➤ EXODUS 21:1, 12–31

1 "Now these are the ordinances which you are to set before them.…

12 "He who strikes a man so that he dies shall surely be put to death.

13 "But if he did not lie in wait *for him,* but God let *him* fall into his hand, then I will appoint you a place to which he may flee.

14 "If, however, a man acts presumptuously toward his neighbor, so as to kill him craftily, you are to take him *even* from My altar, that he may die.

15 "And he who strikes his father or his mother shall surely be put to death.

16 "And he who kidnaps a man, whether he sells him or he is found in his possession, shall surely be put to death.

17 "And he who curses his father or his mother shall surely be put to death.

18 "And if men have a quarrel and one strikes the other with a stone or with *his* fist, and he does not die but remains in bed;

19 if he gets up and walks around outside on his staff, then he who struck him shall go unpunished; he shall only pay for his loss of time, and shall take care of him until he is completely healed.

20 "And if a man strikes his male or female slave with a rod and he dies at his hand, he shall be punished.

21 "If, however, he survives a day or two, no vengeance shall be taken; for he is his property.

22 "And *if* men struggle with each other and strike a woman with child

so that she has a miscarriage, yet there is no *further* injury, he shall surely be fined as the woman's husband may demand of him; and he shall pay as the judges *decide*.

23 "But if there is *any further* injury, then you shall appoint *as a penalty* life for life,

24 eye for eye, tooth for tooth, hand for hand, foot for foot,

25 burn for burn, wound for wound, bruise for bruise.

26 "And if a man strikes the eye of his male or female slave, and destroys it, he shall let him go free on account of his eye.

27 "And if he knocks out a tooth of his male or female slave, he shall let him go free on account of his tooth.

28 "And if an ox gores a man or a woman to death, the ox shall surely be stoned and its flesh shall not be eaten; but the owner of the ox shall go unpunished.

29 "If, however, an ox was previously in the habit of goring, and its owner has been warned, yet he does not confine it, and it kills a man or a woman, the ox shall be stoned and its owner also shall be put to death.

30 "If a ransom is demanded of him, then he shall give for the redemption of his life whatever is demanded of him.

31 "Whether it gores a son or a daughter, it shall be done to him according to the same rule."

1. As you read these ordinances laid down by God, do they seem reasonable or unreasonable? What do you think about them? Are they fair? Would you like to live under them? Why?

2. What verses in this passage was Jesus quoting?

Now let's see what Leviticus 24:17–22 says.

➤ LEVITICUS 24:17–22

17 "And if a man takes the life of any human being, he shall surely be put to death.

18 "And the one who takes the life of an animal shall make it good, life for life.

19 "And if a man injures his neighbor, just as he has done, so it shall be done to him:

20 fracture for fracture, eye for eye, tooth for tooth; just as he has injured a man, so it shall be inflicted on him.

21 "Thus the one who kills an animal shall make it good, but the one who kills a man shall be put to death.

22 "There shall be one standard for you; it shall be for the stranger as well as the native, for I am the LORD your God."

3. Did you gain any new insights from this passage? If so write them down.

So you can get a broader scope of God's law you also need to see what Deuteronomy 19:10–21 says. As you read this passage, mark the following words, each in their own distinctive way: *blood, purge, witness* or *witnesses.*

➤ DEUTERONOMY 19:10–21

10 "So innocent blood will not be shed in the midst of your land which the LORD your God gives you as an inheritance, and bloodguiltiness be on you.

11 "But if there is a man who hates his neighbor and lies in wait for him and rises up against him and strikes him so that he dies, and he flees to one of these cities,

12 then the elders of his city shall send and take him from there and deliver him into the hand of the avenger of blood, that he may die.

13 "You shall not pity him, but you shall purge the blood of the innocent from Israel, that it may go well with you.

14 "You shall not move your neighbor's boundary mark, which the ancestors have set, in your inheritance which you shall inherit in the land that the LORD your God gives you to possess.

15 "A single witness shall not rise up against a man on account of any iniquity or any sin which he has committed; on the evidence of two or three witnesses a matter shall be confirmed.

16 "If a malicious witness rises up against a man to accuse him of wrongdoing,

17 then both the men who have the dispute shall stand before the LORD, before the priests and the judges who will be *in office* in those days.

18 "And the judges shall investigate thoroughly; and if the witness is a false witness *and* he has accused his brother falsely,

19 then you shall do to him just as he had intended to do to his brother. Thus you shall purge the evil from among you.

20 "And the rest will hear and be afraid, and will never again do such an evil thing among you.

21 "Thus you shall not show pity: life for life, eye for eye, tooth for tooth, hand for hand, foot for foot."

4. Make a list of everything you observe and learn from marking the following words in the text:

Blood:

Purge:

Witness:

5. Why do you think God set up these laws? Do you have any quarrel with them? (Sounds rather presumptuous even to ask this question, doesn't it?) If so, what and why?

How does the judicial system that God set up then compare with ours today? The two seem to be opposites, don't they? In biblical days the innocent were protected, whereas today the guilty are. Often in our society the guilty do not get "like" payment. Have you ever wondered what would happen if we started reinstituting capital punishment *without exception or delay* when one has been clearly proven to be a murderer?

Did you notice that under God's judicial system no man would ever be sentenced because of the testimony of a single witness? The testimonies of two or three witnesses were required. God also called the judges to investigate the cases thoroughly and to deal swift retribution to those who gave false testimony. But in our society if someone comes against us and accuses us falsely, it may cost tens of thousands of dollars to defend ourselves. And even if we are successful in our defense, the false accuser walks away, scot-free.

"Life for life, eye for eye, tooth for tooth, hand for hand, foot for foot" certainly would keep people from getting far more than the injury is worth. So many times today people go to court to get all they can. They don't want justice, they want *vengeance*. Many are motivated by pure greed.

As you probably have already seen, God's way of justice did several things. First, it protected against unjust retribution, getting more or taking more than was fair. This is good, isn't it? Many times, because of a man's sinful nature, he is determined to make the guilty one pay through the teeth for what was done. Anger rises and takes control of his reasoning. He wants vengeance and more! Can't you see the benefit of the "eye for an eye" principle?

Even the heathen felt that "an eye for an eye, and a tooth for a tooth" was a just retribution. We see this in Judges 1:6–7:

> But Adoni-bezek fled; and they pursued and caught him and cut off his thumbs and big toes. And Adoni-bezek said, "Seventy kings with their thumbs and their big toes cut off used to gather up *scraps* under my table; as I have done, so God has repaid me." So they brought him to Jerusalem and he died there.

Can you imagine how such a principle of law would benefit society?

FIRST...

Because the punishment was already set, it would curb the indignation of a judge who got so involved in a case that he would bring an unjust retribution against the guilty party. On the other side of the coin, it would keep a judge from showing partiality or from being bribed to give a lesser sentence.

SECOND...

If I decided to take out your eye, I would first have to ponder the fact that if I ever got caught, I would lose my own eye in turn! If I decided that I would take a man's life, I would first have to consider that I would surely and quickly lose my own life if I were caught. And what's more, if I was convicted and put to death for murder, it's a sure bet that I would never murder again! What a deterrent this would be to violent crime! Surely, potential criminals and assailants would think twice.

THIRD...

This law holds man accountable for his behavior, doesn't it? Yet man doesn't want to be held accountable. If he can't get away with breaking the law, what does he want? He wants mercy, yet he was not merciful! Think about it, and we will consider these matters further tomorrow.

DAY   TWO

Why was the law — "an eye for an eye, a tooth for a tooth" — given? I gave you several reasons yesterday. Today I want to give you another.

It was a law to protect innocent people from ungodly, sinful men and women. In order to understand why you are to turn the other cheek, go the second mile, or give away your coat when someone asks for your shirt, you must understand this principle: God is not making the Law void when He tells you to turn the other cheek. Rather, He is calling you to a higher law.

But we know that the Law is good, if one uses it lawfully, realizing the fact that law is not made for a righteous man, but for those who are lawless and rebellious, for the ungodly and sinners, for the unholy and profane, for those who kill their fathers or mothers, for murderers and immoral men and homosexuals and kidnappers and liars and perjurers, and whatever else is contrary to sound teaching. (1 Timothy 1:8–10)

The Law, then, is for *ungodly* men and women. Any time a judicial system changes to the point where it protects the guilty and lets them go free, or allows them to pay a lesser punishment than the magnitude of their crime deserves, lawlessness is encouraged. That judicial system is no longer a protector of the innocent.

It's evident, isn't it, that this is where our system has gone wrong? This is why lawlessness abounds in our land. By clinging to our own humanistic philosophies, we are destroying ourselves and our society.

Do you remember Galatians 3:23? "Before faith came, we were kept in custody under the law." The word for *custody* was a military term that meant to guard as a garrison, or to block the way to escape. The law — an eye for an eye and a tooth for a tooth — was meant to deter red-hot anger that would strike out against the life or limb of another human being. O, that Ecclesiastes 8:11 would be remembered in our courts of law!

Because the sentence against an evil deed is not executed quickly, therefore the hearts of the sons of men among them are given fully to do evil.

The law of retribution was good. It was a law from God, and it was not to be annulled. The only problem was that it had been perverted by the scribes and the Pharisees. "An eye for an eye, and a tooth for a tooth" had been wrested from the judicial level and placed on an individual level. The scribes and Pharisees insisted on personal retribution.

So what is Jesus saying with regard to this law? He is *not* saying that it's a bad principle. He is simply telling us that righteous men are to be controlled by a higher law.

The law of love.

Jesus is calling for love, not legalism. Love has always been the true intent of the Law. Let's look at some scriptures that demonstrate this truth.

1. Read Mark 12:28–34, printed out for you, and then in your own words explain how these verses show that love is the true basis of the Law.

28 And one of the scribes came and heard them arguing, and recognizing that He had answered them well, asked Him, "What commandment is the foremost of all?"

29 Jesus answered, "The foremost is, 'HEAR, O ISRAEL; THE LORD OUR GOD IS ONE LORD;

30 AND YOU SHALL LOVE THE LORD YOUR GOD WITH ALL YOUR HEART, AND WITH ALL YOUR SOUL, AND WITH ALL YOUR MIND, AND WITH ALL YOUR STRENGTH.'

31 "The second is this, 'YOU SHALL LOVE YOUR NEIGHBOR AS YOURSELF.' There is no other commandment greater than these."

32 And the scribe said to Him, "Right, Teacher, You have truly stated that HE IS ONE; AND THERE IS NO ONE ELSE BESIDES HIM;

33 AND TO LOVE HIM WITH ALL THE HEART AND WITH ALL THE UNDERSTANDING AND WITH ALL THE STRENGTH, AND TO LOVE ONE'S NEIGHBOR AS HIMSELF, is much more than all burnt offerings and sacrifices."

34 And when Jesus saw that he had answered intelligently, He said to him, "You are not far from the kingdom of God." And after that, no one would venture to ask Him any more questions.

2. Now read Romans 13:8–10 and summarize in your own words what is said.

Owe nothing to anyone except to love one another; for he who loves his neighbor has fulfilled *the* law. For this, "YOU SHALL NOT COMMIT ADULTERY, YOU SHALL NOT MURDER, YOU SHALL NOT STEAL, YOU

SHALL NOT COVET," and if there is any other commandment, it is summed up in this saying, "YOU SHALL LOVE YOUR NEIGHBOR AS YOURSELF." Love does no wrong to a neighbor; love therefore is the fulfillment of *the* law.

3. Now look at 1 Corinthians 13. Read verses 1–8, and write down what verse 7 says about love.

¹ If I speak with the tongues of men and of angels, but do not have love, I have become a noisy gong or a clanging cymbal.

² And if I have *the gift of* prophecy, and know all mysteries and all knowledge; and if I have all faith, so as to remove mountains, but do not have love, I am nothing.

³ And if I give all my possessions to feed *the poor,* and if I deliver my body to be burned, but do not have love, it profits me nothing.

⁴ Love is patient, love is kind, *and* is not jealous; love does not brag *and* is not arrogant,

⁵ does not act unbecomingly; it does not seek its own, is not provoked, does not take into account a wrong *suffered,*

⁶ does not rejoice in unrighteousness, but rejoices with the truth;

⁷ bears all things, believes all things, hopes all things, endures all things.

⁸ Love never fails; but if *there are gifts of* prophecy, they will be done away; if *there are* tongues, they will cease; if *there is* knowledge, it will be done away.

In Romans 13:10 we saw that love is "the fulfillment of the law." Since it is, love does not have to demand an eye for an eye, and a tooth for a tooth. It realizes that the major purpose of that Law was twofold: to protect a person against unjust retribution and to cause a man to think twice before committing a crime.

For this reason, the Law can still be fulfilled by love turning its cheek. This demonstrates before the world, once again, the reality of God in us as He was in Christ: "Reconciling the world to Himself, not counting their trespasses against them" (2 Corinthians 5:19).

O Beloved, do you see it? If we are to be perfect as our Father in heaven is perfect, we have to reach beyond the legalism of the Law to its true intent...which is love.

We have something to show those who would insult us, seek our possessions, or abuse our privileges. Before a watching world, we must demonstrate that because Christ is in us, we will go beyond the just letter of the Law and will respond with the very grace of God. We are not going to count their trespasses against them, but we will turn the other cheek, give our coats, go the extra mile, and not turn away from the one who wants to borrow from us.

What will this demonstrate to a watching world?

The meekness of Jesus.

The mercy of God.

The goodness of God

...which leads men to repentance (Romans 2:4).

Matthew 5:38–42 is not teaching the doctrine of pacifism. It has nothing to do with nation going to war against nation. We cannot take these verses to Congress and say, "If we would simply do this and respond this way to aggressors who seek to take control of our country, God would be with us." That would be national suicide! It would also be taking a message intended for an individual and trying to apply it to a nation. This verse belongs to Christians, not judicial systems or nations.

What then? Are we to keep turning the other cheek until we are battered to death? Are we to keep giving away our possessions until we're in debt ourselves? I don't believe that is what God is saying here. Whenever you turn the other cheek, or give away your coat, or walk an extra mile, or give to the one who wants to borrow, you must remember that you are doing it out of *love*. Love is the true intent of our Lord's words. And love always desires another's highest good. If an alcoholic, then, pleads for money to buy a bottle of cheap wine, offer to buy him a hot meal instead!

What God is telling us, in essence, is that love does not demand its rights. It does not ask for a just reward. Love is always merciful. It looks beyond the immediate to another's eternal good.

What have you learned, Beloved, for your life? How can you apply the things you have learned these last two days to your daily walk? Summarize it in a sentence or two in the space below...and then talk to God about it.

DAY   THREE

As a new Christian, I once read a thought-provoking little tract entitled "Others May, You Cannot." The essence of its message was the higher calling of those who would follow Christ wholeheartedly. It pointed out that while some things might be lawful or permissible for the Christian, things to which the Bible doesn't specifically speak, those who wish to live on the highest plane may heed God's call and choose to leave these things alone.

In Matthew 5:38–48, God is calling us to a very high plane of life.

He is calling us to live beyond the letter of the Law.

He is calling us to catch the spirit of the Law.

He is taking us beyond a legalism that wants to know "how far it can go," to a love that never considers itself at all.

Let's read the passage again, before we proceed any further.

➤ MATTHEW 5:38–48

38 "You have heard that it was said, 'AN EYE FOR AN EYE, AND A TOOTH FOR A TOOTH.'

39 "But I say to you, do not resist him who is evil; but whoever slaps you on your right cheek, turn to him the other also.

40 "And if anyone wants to sue you, and take your shirt, let him have your coat also.

41 "And whoever shall force you to go one mile, go with him two.

42 "Give to him who asks of you, and do not turn away from him who wants to borrow from you.

43 "You have heard that it was said, 'YOU SHALL LOVE YOUR NEIGHBOR, and hate your enemy.'

44 "But I say to you, love your enemies, and pray for those who persecute you

45 in order that you may be sons of your Father who is in heaven; for He causes His sun to rise on *the* evil and *the* good, and sends rain on *the* righteous and *the* unrighteous.

46 "For if you love those who love you, what reward have you? Do not even the tax-gatherers do the same?

47 "And if you greet your brothers only, what do you do more *than others?* Do not even the Gentiles do the same?

48 "Therefore you are to be perfect, as your heavenly Father is perfect."

Love does not seek personal justice. Therefore if anyone wants to sue you and take your shirt, love says, "Here, take my coat also." Love will give up its rights in order to demonstrate the character of God. Why? Because love lives on a higher plane.

It's not easy up there on that "higher plane," is it? It separates you from others. It lets people take advantage of you. But then…what's new? Don't people take advantage of God? Yes, they take advantage of Him, but it never alters His character. And like Him, our character is never to be altered by those who respond to us. Does that bear repeating? *My character is never to be altered by another's response to me.*

Love does not cling to its personal possessions. Therefore, love gives to him who asks and does not turn away the one who wants to borrow. Love expands itself. Love gives the ultimate, and in its giving disarms the receiver. Love even loves its enemies and in compassion prays for those who persecute it. Love cannot restrain its affection...not if it is God's love!

Love lives on a higher plane.

If you are going to turn the other cheek, give away your coat, go the second mile, give to him who asks, and love your enemies, then it logically follows that you cannot be occupied or concerned with self. Of course, as you already know, this is meekness personified. Meekness is not occupied with self at all. It does not consider retaliation in any form.

During the time of our Lord, Roman soldiers overran Israel. A Roman soldier could compel a civilian to carry his burden the distance of one mile, but no more. The law was designed to keep the soldier from taking advantage of the civilian. Since righteousness is to be practical, Jesus addressed the current situation of His day, and in doing so gave all of us a practical illustration. Love shoulders that burden and walks beyond the required 5,280 feet. It goes beyond what it is compelled to do. Love lives on a higher plane than the Law.

The Jews were told that they were to love their neighbors and hate their enemies (Matthew 5:43). Note that I said "told," for nowhere does the Word distinctly say they are to hate their enemies. God did say to King Jehoshaphat, "Should you help the wicked and love those who hate the LORD and so *bring* wrath on yourself from the LORD?" (2 Chronicles 19:2).

What the Pharisees told the people regarding loving their neighbors and hating their enemies could have been the scribes' and the Pharisees' interpretation of Leviticus 19:18: "You shall not take vengeance, nor bear any grudge against the sons of your people, but you shall love your neighbor as yourself; I am the LORD." From that they may have deduced that they were to love only their neighbors — and were allowed to hate their enemies.

This is why Jesus had to tell them the parable of the good Samaritan, a parable prompted by a man who wished to justify himself by saying to Jesus, "And who is my neighbor?" (Luke 10:29). Through the parable of the good Samaritan, Jesus taught him that a neighbor is anyone in need.

Loving our neighbors as ourselves, then, means we are to love all men as we love ourselves. When God sent Jesus to die for us, He sent Jesus to die for the whole world: "God so loved the world, that He gave His only begotten Son…" (John 3:16). Jesus is "the propitiation for our sins; and not for ours only, but also for *those of* the whole world" (1 John 2:2). Love does not discriminate because God does not discriminate.

I have never forgotten a few lines of Shakespeare that I memorized in high school:

Let me not to the marriage of true minds
Admit impediments. Love is not love
Which alters when it alteration finds,
Or bends with the remover to remove.
Oh, no! it is an ever-fixed mark,
That looks on tempests and is never shaken.…

If you are going to be perfect as your heavenly Father is perfect, you must not alter when you alteration find. Your love must be perfected "in order that you may be sons of your Father who is in heaven; for He causes His sun to rise on *the* evil and *the* good, and sends rain on *the* righteous and *the* unrighteous. For if you love those who love you, what reward have you?" (Matthew 5:45–46).

You and I, Beloved, cannot live the way others live. We must live on love's highest plane. Our love does "more than others."

Others may, you cannot.

O Beloved, do you see what God expects of you? Do you see how high your calling is? Do you truly see what it means to be the very sons and daughters of the Most High God?

In Acts 1:8 when Jesus says, "You shall be my witnesses," the word *witnesses* in the Greek is similar to the English word *martyr,* one willing to lay down his life. That's what God is calling us to do in Matthew 5:38–48. God laid down His life in the person of His Son for all mankind. Some would believe and respond; others would trample on that divine love. It did not matter. Love was willing to be trampled.

So what do you do? You:

"Bless those who persecute you; bless and curse not."

"Never pay back evil for evil to anyone."

"Never take your own revenge."

"If your enemy is hungry, feed him, and if he is thirsty, give him a drink."

"Overcome evil with good."

"Owe nothing to anyone except to love one another."

(Romans 12:14, 17, 19, 20, 21; 13:8).

Will you live on the highest plane? Do you and I really have a choice?

DAY   FOUR

Today as we begin Matthew 6, I have a special assignment in mind for you.

During our study together, I want to keep giving you principles of Bible study that will add stability and security to your life. Without these principles, we are in danger of being "children, tossed here and there by waves, and carried about by every wind of doctrine, by the trickery of men, by craftiness in deceitful scheming" (Ephesians 4:14).

I think you might find the following exercise both profitable and a refreshing change of pace. If you will look in the back of the book at the Sermon on the Mount printed there in full, you will notice that some verse numbers are in bolder type than others. This marks the beginning of a new paragraph. Your assignment for today is to read through Matthew 6, paragraph by paragraph. As you do, pick out one or two words that best describe what each paragraph is about; then write that word next to the verse which divides it from the next paragraph.

When you have finished, write in the space below the truth that spoke to you the most. Then spend some time in prayer, asking God to show you any way that you are practicing your righteousness to be seen by others, rather than to be seen by the eyes of your Father alone.

Did you find yourself prodded or pierced by the truth as you considered these things? I understand, Beloved. I, too, have been prodded and pierced. Yet I have also been brought to my knees in weeping and confession, and the cleansing has been wonderful. The Sermon on the Mount has created within me such a hunger and such a thirst for a deeper righteousness! I pray, Beloved, that God is blessing you in the same way.

I love you with the love of the Lord. Have a good day.

DAY   FIVE

As you read through Matthew 6 yesterday, you observed that Jesus was giving His listeners some very specific instructions. In verse 2, for example, He said, "When you give alms...." In verse 5 He said, "When you pray...." Then down in verse 16 He said, "And whenever you fast...."

As we begin our final day of study this week, read through Matthew 6 and 7. As you read, watch for any warnings such as "beware" and instructions such as "do not...." Sometimes the "do not" is followed with a "but." It will help your learning process to mark these phrases in some distinctive way, not only in this book but in your own Bible. As you mark each of these warnings and/or instructions, you will get an overview of the content of these chapters.

Jesus' first "beware" in His sermon occurs in Matthew 6:1 where He tells his listeners to beware of practicing their righteousness to be noticed by men.

It's hard, isn't it, not to want or seek the approval of others? I know. I've been there and this is an area I must watch very carefully. Approbation is something we all love...and in a sense need. Yet as disciples of Christ, Jesus moves us to a new plane...the higher plane of living for one ultimate purpose — to bring Him pleasure. How we need to "have as our ambition, whether at home or absent, to be pleasing to Him" (2 Corinthians 5:9).

To maintain this we need to ask the same question Paul asked — and come to the same conclusion:

For am I now seeking the favor of men, or of God? Or am I striving to please men? If I were still trying to please men, I would not be a bond-servant of Christ. (Galatians 1:10)

Our approval is to come from God. And if that is so, then we must do what we do for Him, not for the reward of praise from others. In this teaching, Jesus touches on some issues where we might find ourselves doing "righteous" acts with very unrighteous motives!

The first of these occurs in the arena of giving.

The Old Testament economy portrays basically three types of giving: tithes, freewill offerings, and gifts to the poor. The last — gifts to the poor, or "almsgiving" — is the type of giving that Jesus deals with in Matthew 6. It was a giving that promised rich blessing from God.

Let's look at several passages so that you can understand the Jewish mentality toward giving and blessing, and the promises God has for you as you give alms to the poor.

1. Deuteronomy 15:7–11 states:

"If there is a poor man with you, one of your brothers, in any of your towns in your land which the LORD your God is giving you, you shall not harden your heart, nor close your hand from your poor brother; but you shall freely open your hand to him, and shall generously lend him sufficient for his need *in* whatever he lacks. Beware, lest there is a base thought in your heart, saying, 'The seventh year, the year of remission, is near,' and your eye is hostile toward your poor brother, and you give him nothing; then he may cry to the LORD against you, and it will be a sin in you. You shall generously give to him, and your heart shall not be grieved when you give to him, because for this thing the LORD your God will bless you in all your work and in all your undertakings. For the poor will never cease *to be* in the land; therefore I command you, saying, 'You shall freely open your hand to your brother, to your needy and poor in your land.'"

What do you learn from these verses about almsgiving?

2. Now then, let's see what we can learn from Proverbs 11:24–25. Read it, and then record what you learn.

There is one who scatters, yet increases all the more,
And there is one who withholds what is justly due, but *it results*
only in want.
The generous man will be prosperous,
And he who waters will himself be watered.
(Proverbs 11:24–25)

3. Blessings that came from giving to the poor were quite varied, as is evident in Psalm 41:1–3. Listen....

How blessed is he who considers the helpless;
The LORD will deliver him in a day of trouble.
The LORD will protect him, and keep him alive,
And he shall be called blessed upon the earth;
And do not give him over to the desire of his enemies.
The LORD will sustain him upon his sickbed;
In his illness, Thou dost restore him to health.

List the various things the Lord promises to do, in this passage, for those who consider the helpless (the poor).

Almsgiving for some people — hypocrites, the Lord calls them — became a vehicle for getting praise, attention, and admiration from others. For this reason, some made a big ceremony out of their giving. Apparently they went so far as to sound trumpets in the synagogues and streets, announcing what they were about to do! Can you imagine? Perhaps these high-profile givers justified the use of the trumpet as a summons to the poor. Perhaps they intended the trumpet to announce: "Come running, you impoverished people! Come partake of my amazing and wonderful benevolence!" After all, if they didn't sound the trumpets, the poor couldn't come running!

We can come up with all sorts of rationalizations for drawing attention to ourselves, can't we? That's why the Lord tells us to "beware!"

Now then, as we bring today's assignment to a close, let's let the Word examine our hearts. Is there any way this warning might apply to you?

When you give to people, or to a ministry with needs, do you do it only if you get your name on a plaque or printed in the bulletin?

Do you love it when certain churches publish lists of those who have met their monthly giving quota? Do you make certain you give so that you will not be embarrassed by the absence of your name from the list?

Will you only give if in some way your giving is going to be recognized?

If that is so, then Matthew 6 says you already have your reward in full. There's no more reward coming. But if when you give alms, you "do not let your left hand know what your right hand is doing that your alms may be in secret" then "your Father who sees in secret will repay you." When do you want your reward, Beloved? Now or later?

Go to the Lord and talk to Him about all that you've read. Share with

Him your fears. He loves to communicate with you in truth. Also, Beloved, examine your motives for giving. Examine your giving. Do you give? Ask God to search your heart and your pocketbook. Many times you can tell the condition of your heart by looking at how you handle your pocketbook!

There is something about our unredeemed flesh that wants to be seen...applauded...praised...appreciated. Jesus knows this. He knows what a stumbling block it can become to us. Therefore, He warns us in Matthew 6:1: "Beware of practicing your righteousness before men to be noticed by them." God wants His children to be aware of the flesh "putting on a show" in order to be seen and applauded by others. This is the way the hypocrites live, and we're not to live that way.

Children of the King must live on a higher plane!

PRAYING AND FASTING GOD'S WAY

Down through the centuries followers of Jesus Christ have cried out, "Lord, teach me to pray!"

His answer has never changed. It is timeless.

And He said to them, "When you pray, say:

'Father, hallowed be Thy name.

Thy kingdom come.

'Give us each day our daily bread.

'And forgive us our sins,

For we ourselves also forgive everyone who is indebted to us.

And lead us not into temptation.'"

(Luke 11:2–4)

Luke records for us Jesus' response to his disciples' request. Back in Matthew, however, we have a more expanded explanation. In His Sermon on the Mount, our Lord not only teaches us *what* to pray, but *how* to pray.

Let's stop and take a careful look at this passage on prayer. Turn to the Sermon on the Mount, and read Matthew 6:1–18. Note how verses 2, 5, and 16 relate to verse 1 in this chapter. Jesus has a warning and a word of exhortation regarding three critical life disciplines: giving, prayer, and fasting. This week we are going to look at the latter two, one at a time.

Printed out for you is Matthew 6:5–15 so you can have the text in this chapter as you study the discipline of prayer. Read it through again, and this time mark every occurrence of the word *pray* and all its synonyms. Also notice each use of the repeated phrase *when you pray* or *when you are praying*. This is a key phrase through which we can discern our Lord's specific instructions regarding prayer. Mark each occurrence in a distinctive way.

➤ MATTHEW 6:5–15

"And when you pray, you are not to be as the hypocrites; for they love to stand and pray in the synagogues and on the street corners, in order to be seen by men. Truly I say to you, they have their reward in full. But you, when you pray, go into your inner room, and when you have shut your door, pray to your Father who is in secret, and your Father who sees in secret will repay you. And when you are praying, do not use meaningless repetition, as the Gentiles do, for they suppose that they will be heard for their many words. Therefore do not be like them; for your Father knows what you need, before you ask Him. Pray, then, in this way:

'Our Father who art in heaven,
Hallowed be Thy name.
'Thy kingdom come.
Thy will be done,
On earth as it is in heaven.
'Give us this day our daily bread.
'And forgive us our debts, as we also have forgiven our debtors.
'And do not lead us into temptation, but deliver us from evil.
[For Thine is the kingdom, and the power, and the glory, forever. Amen].'

"For if you forgive men for their transgressions, your heavenly Father will also forgive you. But if you do not forgive men, then your Father will not forgive your transgressions."

Take a minute or two to list a few of Jesus' instructions about prayer in this passage. At this point, don't go into too much detail on the Lord's prayer. We'll spend time together on these wonderful verses a little later.

Once again, Jesus tells His listeners that they are not to pray as the hypocrites, to be seen by men. If the hypocrites were going to get man's praise for their prayers, then they had to pray in public. Apparently, from Jesus' admonition, hypocrites were indeed praying in public — but not in private.

When and where do you pray, Beloved — and why?

If you are only praying to be seen by others, then you probably do more praying in public than in private. And what does Jesus say? His instruction on private prayer is very clear. You need to be alone. Does that mean, then, that we are not to pray in public nor participate in public prayer meetings? I don't think so, for the Word of God has many other references to public praying. I don't believe Jesus' purpose was to condemn public prayer but to show us that true prayer is for communication between God and the individual — not for impressing others with our piety.

Dwight Pentecost in his book *The Sermon on the Mount* puts it so well.

Two who are in love require privacy to properly communicate. Little real communication is possible in public. Volumes can be communicated in moments when there is privacy. In the busyness of life, communication with the Father is impossible unless there is privacy. That's why the Lord said if we are to communicate with the Father we must go to our room and shut the door. One prying eye can spoil communication. As soon as we are conscious of one observer, the privacy necessary to intimately communicate is gone, and we become conscious of the observer rather than the Father with whom we are talking. Therefore, the Pharisees could not communicate with the Father when they gathered an audience to hear their prayers. Prayer is private communication.[1]

Because prayer is private communication, does this mean we can never carry on this communication publicly with God? Oh no, Beloved. Public prayer *can* be private communication if our hearts are united, if we are aware that we have come into the presence of God and are actually praying and worshiping Him as a body. Yet we must always remember to Whom we are speaking! Genuine prayer is for God, not other people.

Reuben A. Torrey, an outstanding Bible teacher in the days of D. L. Moody, wrote *The Power of Prayer*. Within those pages he makes this observation.

We should never utter one syllable of prayer, either in public or in private, until we are definitely conscious that we have come into the presence of God and are actually praying to him.... I can remember when that thought transformed my prayer life. I was brought up to pray. I was taught to pray so early in life that I have not the slightest recollection of who taught me to pray.... Nevertheless, prayer was largely a mere matter of form. There was little real thought of God, and no real approach to God. And even after I was converted, yes, even after I had entered the ministry, prayer was largely a matter of form. But the day came when I realized what real prayer meant, realized that prayer was having an audience with God, actually coming into the presence of God and asking and getting things from Him. And the realization of that fact transformed my prayer life. Before that, prayer had been a mere duty, and sometimes a very irksome duty, but from that time on prayer has been not merely a duty but a privilege, one of the most highly esteemed privileges of life. Before that, the thought that I had was, "How much time must I spend in prayer?" The thought that now possesses me is, "How much time may I spend in prayer without neglecting the other privileges and duties of life?"[2]

Isn't this what Jesus is saying to us in Matthew 5? Pray when you are conscious of God's presence, for the purpose of prayer is to communicate with God, not to be seen by the watching eyes of others.

Prayer and consistent study of the Word of God are both essential if you are going to sustain a vital relationship with Almighty God. They are twin keys, keys that go to two locks on the door to the abundant life which He has promised. And both must be used in order to open the door. Why? Because both involve communion with God. If one is lacking, the other will be affected. Right now, you are in the process of letting God communicate with you through His Word, so let's see what we can learn about the other side of that vital communication.

Prayer is communicating with your Father about every matter of life, a discipline which not only sustains you but brings confidence and quietness to your soul as you confront the complexities of daily living. Prayer is the Christian's compass, giving the child of God direction for the course of his or her life. If exercised according to the Word of God, prayer is a discipline which gets you alone with God, where you can focus on Him and Him alone.

As we will see tomorrow, prayer can follow a certain pattern. At the same time, however, it is not to be the repetition of meaningless words. Jesus makes this very clear in Matthew 6:7 when He tells His disciples that they are not to use meaningless repetition. Prayer is to be an honest, heartfelt communication between you and your heavenly Father. Saying a lot of words or jumping through the hoops of some set formula is not what God desires from you. When you pray, you are simply talking to your Father...a Father who knows what you need before you ever ask! You are coming to the One who delights to "give what is good to those who ask Him" (Matthew 7:11).

Now then, my friend, why don't you take what you have observed in this text of Matthew 6 and put it into practice. Take a long walk, or shut the door to your room, or do whatever you have to do to get alone where you can be quiet and undisturbed before Him.

Tell your Father you want to be with Him.

Sit or kneel before Him, and thank Him for His presence.

Then talk to Him, beginning with reflecting on who He is. From there, see where He leads you in your conversation.

Why delay? Your Father is waiting.

DAY   TWO

As Luke 11 opens, Jesus has just finished praying.

He may have been praying silently, His lips moving in fervent supplication. Or He might have been praying out loud, calling on His Father and praising His name. Scripture doesn't tell us *how* Jesus was praying, but it is apparent that His disciples saw or heard something that touched them or intrigued them. As soon as Jesus concluded His prayer, one of His disciples approached Him and said, "Lord, teach us to pray...."

His response to their request is recorded for time and eternity because it would never change. Down through the centuries, it has remained the same. From age to age. From culture to culture. From nation to nation.

"When you pray, say:
'Father, hallowed be Thy name.
Thy kingdom come.
'Give us each day our daily bread.
'And forgive us our sins,
For we ourselves also forgive everyone who is indebted to us.
And lead us not into temptation.'"
(Luke 11:2–4)

In the days of our Lord, there were no printing presses, no plethora of books. For this reason it was customary for rabbis to give their disciples a collection of brief sentences — reminders — which would trigger what they were to remember.

These were called "index sentences" and would be used to lead their students deeper into vital subject areas. Some scholars believe that the Lord's Prayer was given to the disciples as a list of index sentences, each one in and of itself a topic for prayer.

What I have learned about the Lord's Prayer as a pattern for my personal praying has absolutely liberated me in this area of my life. By using this pattern I have found that whether I have fifteen minutes or an hour for prayer in the morning, I am able to cover the spectrum of subjects which Jesus teaches are vital to communication with God. The emphasis of my prayers varies, of course, according to the time I have and how He chooses to lead me. Having more time will always give more depth and breadth to my prayer. Yet whether the time is long or short, this pattern has helped me to become more balanced and comprehensive in my praying. It has been more satisfying, too.

Since each sentence of what you and I refer to as "the Lord's Prayer" touches on a topic or subject to be covered in prayer, I would like you to look at the Lord's Prayer sentence by sentence. Write out as briefly as possible the topic you think each sentence covers.

The prayer is printed out for you, sentence by sentence. So take it one sentence at a time, and see what you come up with.

_____1. Our Father who art in heaven, hallowed be Thy name.

_____2. Thy Kingdom come.

_____3. Thy will be done, on earth as it is in heaven.

_____4. Give us this day our daily bread.

_____5. And forgive us our debts, as we also have forgiven our debtors.

_____*6. And do not lead us into temptation, but deliver us from evil.

_____*7. For Thine is the kingdom, and the power, and the glory, forever. Amen.

*You may want to consider 6 and 7 as one sentence, which is fine, or you may consider them separately.

In his book *Prayer*, Samuel Zwemer writes that the Lord's Prayer contains:

> Every possible desire of the praying heart. It contains a whole world of spiritual requirements, and combines in simple language every divine promise, every human sorrow and want in every Christian aspiration for the good of others.

James Boice writes in *The Sermon on the Mount*:

> The greatest minds of the Christian church have always known this, and as a result the Lord's Prayer has been used throughout centuries as an outline for countless expositions of the nature of prayer and Christian doctrine.

Andrew Murray, in *With Christ in the School of Prayer,* said that the Lord's Prayer is

> ...a form of prayer that becomes the model and inspiration for all other prayer, and yet always draws us back to itself as the deepest utterance of our souls before God.

If you read through the Lord's Prayer as six topical sentences, the topics would fall in this order:

1. worship
2. allegiance
3. submission
4. petition
5. confession
6. deliverance.

Or, if you see seven topical sentences, then the last might be a return to worship, a heartfelt acknowledgment of His sovereignty, omnipotence.

When I first followed this exercise, however, I felt that something was missing in this prayer. *Where was intercession?* Where was the vital necessity of seeking God on the behalf of others?

As I went back to the text with this question in mind, I suddenly saw what I had missed before. Intercession is indeed a part of this model prayer...and it occurs in every "our," "we," and "us." To pray through this prayer is not to pray for myself alone but also on behalf of those who belong to the body of Jesus Christ:

> give *us* this day *our* daily bread...
>
> forgive us *our* debts...
>
> do not lead *us* into temptation...
>
> deliver *us* from evil.

"But wait," you might say. "What about intercession for those who are lost? Isn't that a part of this 'model prayer'?"

If that is your concern, I'm thankful! It shows that you know how vital prayer is in bringing men, women, and children into the kingdom of heaven. Intercession for the salvation of others *is* covered in one of the index sentences. I will point it out as we move through this prayer, sentence by sentence.

As we progress through this abbreviated study of the Lord's Prayer, I want you to realize that this is simply a cursory observation of truths that must be mined diligently from the whole counsel of God on prayer. These sentences are like rich coal mines that have enough coal to ignite your heart in triumphant worship and confident petition. And these few pages of study on prayer are only a beginning! If you would like to pursue this subject further, I have written a four-week study entitled *Lord, Teach Me to Pray...in 28 Days*. It is published by Harvest House and may be obtained from your local bookstore or ordered through Precept Ministries.

Now then, let's look at Jesus' way to pray, one sentence at a time.

"OUR FATHER WHO ART IN HEAVEN, HALLOWED BE THY NAME..."

The first index sentence lays the foundation for everything which follows. It calls us into the presence of the One who alone is worthy of our praise and adoration. It brings us before the Sovereign of the universe, who can meet our needs and satisfy the deepest longings of our hearts. To me, worship is the act of looking at God's Word in order to focus on who God is. The Word of God gives us the perfect revelation of who He is, making worship the basis of all true prayer. "He who comes to God must believe that He is, and *that* He is a rewarder of those who seek Him" (Hebrews 11:6).

What is our relationship to this God whom we worship? It is nothing less than that of a child to his Father. "Father." Can you imagine calling Jehovah, the self-existing, sovereign God, "Father"? To an Old Testament Jew, calling God "Father" would have been unthinkable!

So with the very first two words of this prayer, Jesus introduced a shocking new concept! *Our Father....* Those words opened up a whole new realm of intimacy, an intimacy that most of Israel never ventured into. Together, we can cry out with John, "See how great a love the Father has bestowed upon us, that we should be called children of God" (1 John 3:1). His Spirit living within us enables us to cry out to Him, *Abba! Father!*

The word that Jesus uses for Father is *Abba,* the term a child used for his daddy and continued to use into adulthood. It's a term you still hear as you walk the streets of Israel. Filled with devotion, love, admiration, confidence, and security, *Abba* contains all the trust of a little child. In this first index sentence, then, we see that prayer is the birthright of those who have been born again — born from above. Prayer is the privilege of the child of God.

The pattern begins with worship, for worship is the cornerstone that sets the foundation for effective prayer. It is the foundation upon which every petition finds its support. In many churches and prayer closets, worship is the missing spark that would ignite hearts in flames of holy devotion and unconditional trust.

In that light, let's do one more thing before we call it a day.

Read 2 Chronicles 20:1–13, which is printed out for you. As you read, note who is speaking, what the circumstances are, and how they are dealt with. Watch to see what part worship plays in this situation.

As you read, mark every reference to God with a triangle like this: and color it yellow. Then, when you finish, in the space provided list everything you learn about God from this passage.

➤ 2 CHRONICLES 20:1–13

Now it came about after this that the sons of Moab and the sons of Ammon, together with some of the Meunites, came to make war against Jehoshaphat. Then some came and reported to Jehoshaphat, saying, "A great multitude is coming against you from beyond the sea, out of Aram and behold, they are in Hazazon-tamar (that is Engedi)." And Jehoshaphat was afraid and turned his attention to seek the LORD; and proclaimed a fast throughout all Judah. So Judah gathered together to seek help from the LORD; they even came from all the cities of Judah to seek the LORD.

Then Jehoshaphat stood in the assembly of Judah and Jerusalem, in the house of the LORD before the new court, and he said, "O LORD, the God of our fathers, art Thou not God in the heavens? And art Thou not ruler over all the kingdoms of the nations? Power and might are in Thy hand so that no one can stand against Thee. Didst Thou not, O our God, drive out the inhabitants of this land before Thy people Israel, and give it to the descendants of Abraham Thy friend forever? And they lived in it, and have built Thee a sanctuary there for Thy name, saying, 'Should evil come upon us, the sword, *or* judgment, or pestilence, or famine, we will stand before this house and before Thee (for Thy name is in this house) and cry to Thee in our distress, and Thou wilt hear and deliver *us*.' And now behold, the sons of Ammon and Moab and Mount Seir, whom Thou didst not let Israel invade when they came out of the land of Egypt (they turned aside from them and did not destroy them), behold *how* they are rewarding us by coming to drive us out from Thy possession which Thou hast given us as an inheritance. O our God, wilt Thou not judge them? For we are powerless before this great multitude who are coming against us; nor do we know what to do, but our eyes are on Thee." And all Judah was standing before the LORD, with their infants, their wives, and their children.

Now, Beloved of God, can you see the role of worship and what the king remembered and reminded God about? Do you think it helped Jehoshaphat to remember these things? How?

As you bring this day's study to a close, do you find yourself in a situation similar to the king's? Is there anything in this passage which might help you as you find an enemy or adverse situation threatening you or someone you love? Take your worries and fears to your Father. Spend time with our *El Elyon* who sits on His sovereign throne in heaven. Hallow, or reverence His name. He is *Elohim*, your Creator. He is *El Shaddai*, your almighty, all-sufficient Father. He is your *El Roi*, the God who sees. He is *Jehovah*, the I AM who as *Jehovah-jireh* has provided all you need through His Lamb. Kneel beneath the banner of your *Jehovah-nissi*, giving Him your allegiance, submitting to your *Adonai* as Lord that you might walk in righteousness as the child of *Jehovah-tsidkenu*. Let *Jehovah-rapha* heal your hurts. Seek the guidance of your shepherd, *Jehovah-raah*, and know that as *Jehovah-shammah*, He is always there. The throne of *Elohim*, the everlasting God, is never vacant. *Jehovah-sabaoth*, who rules over the hosts of heaven, awaits your worship.[3]

DAY   THREE

"THY KINGDOM COME..."

The second index sentence in the Lord's Prayer shows our allegiance to God and to His kingdom. Had Jesus not given us the third index sentence, "Thy will be done, on earth as it is in heaven," this sentence would cover the topic adequately. For after all, if I'm going to give my allegiance, then I'm going to be willing to submit to His will.

In the first index sentence our focus is upon God. We see Him as the

Sovereign One ruling from heaven. Through various scriptures we catch a glimpse of how wonderful heaven must be, where His will is not questioned or thwarted in any way but carried out with total obedience. Having seen God, having reverenced Him because His name reveals Him as He really is, is it not logical that we would bow the knee and say to Him, "Father, we want Your kingdom to come"?

Here is our opportunity to affirm daily our allegiance to His kingdom, acknowledging we have but one God, and He must rule today above all else. Here is our opportunity in prayer to expedite the coming of His literal kingdom to earth. The great Shepherd of the sheep cannot come until all of the sheep are inside the fold. This index sentence has the effect, then, of drawing us into intercession for those outside the kingdom of God. When we pray "Thy kingdom come," we are praying that Jesus' lost sheep would hear His voice, come to Him, and receive eternal life.

As I pray these words, remembering the lost, I often pray Acts 26:18, asking God to "open their eyes so that they may turn from darkness to light and from the dominion of Satan to God, in order that they may receive forgiveness of sins and an inheritance among those who have been sanctified by faith in [Jesus]."

If you and I could catch a glimpse of how crucial our prayers are in preparing people's hearts to receive the seed of God's Word, I believe we would spend much more time on our knees! That's where effective evangelism begins.

"THY WILL BE DONE..."

After we profess our allegiance by praying for His kingdom to come, it is logical and reasonable that we would pray "Thy will be done."

Before you bring any petition before God's throne, before your prayers can ever be effective, *you must submit to the will of God.* This is the purpose of the third index sentence. John 9:31 tells us that God does not hear sinners, but if anyone fears God and does His will, then God hears him.

In the pattern of the Lord's Prayer, petition follows on the heels of submission. The order cannot be reversed! After all, how can we expect God to grant us our desires when we refuse to submit to His will, whatever it is?

Submission to the will of God is the key to the storehouse of answered prayer. "And this is the confidence which we have before Him, that, if we ask anything *according to His will*, He hears us. And if we know that He hears us in whatever we ask, we know that we have the requests which we have asked from Him" (1 John 5:14–15, italics added). If you would know the will of God, you must understand the Word of God! The will of God and the Word of God go together. They cannot be separated, for through His Word we are sure of His will. Jesus puts it very succinctly:

> "If you abide in Me, and My words abide in you, ask whatever you wish, and it shall be done for you." (John 15:7)

"GIVE US THIS DAY OUR DAILY BREAD…"

The next index sentence is one of petition. As a child you have come to your Father. As a child it is only right that your Father meet your needs. Yet notice where this index sentence falls in our Lord's Prayer. Petition comes *after* we have worshiped our Father, given Him our allegiance, and submitted to His will. Then and only then are we spiritually ready to ask Him to supply our needs.

These first three index sentences put us in the context of petition, for the promises of God regarding asking and receiving are always qualified by asking in His name — or in accordance with His name. Our petitions then must coincide with *who He is* and with *who we are* as children of God. How vital it is that we understand this! It will keep us from hastily and thoughtlessly grabbing and claiming a verse like John 14:13:

> "And whatever you ask in My name, that will I do, that the Father may be glorified in the Son."

It's no wonder we find ourselves confused and disappointed, wondering "why God doesn't do what He said He would do." Some have taken John 14:13 as *carte blanche* to ask for whatever their hearts desire without stopping to realize that whatever we ask must be asked in His name. And if I am asking for something in His name, then I am also asking for something in accordance with His character. Remember the pattern of prayer? It begins with "hallowed be Thy name." Reverence for His name is what governs our petitions.

Petitions for what? For when?

It's interesting to me that the petition is "give us this day our daily bread."

God keeps us coming to Him day by day, doesn't He? This isn't a petition for next week's bread. It isn't a request for the coming year. It's a petition for the *daily* needs of life. I believe Jesus uses the term *bread* because it was considered the staff of life. Bread symbolically covers all of our physical needs, those things that are necessary to sustain our lives. Oh, there is so much I could say here, Beloved, but we have to move on. I pray that God will use these words to make you hunger to study more and more about this subject of prayer. It is your birthright!

"FORGIVE US OUR DEBTS, AS WE ALSO HAVE FORGIVEN OUR DEBTORS..."

The next index sentence is a cry to God for forgiveness. Yet it is a forgiveness that is linked to our forgiveness of others.

Why do I say that? Because of one little, two-letter word — *as*.

Back in the Beatitudes of Matthew 5, Jesus teaches us that receiving mercy is related to being merciful. In the same way, this index sentence teaches that we ask for forgiveness in accordance with our forgiveness of others.

Some people find this very difficult. It's hard for them to comprehend that God would withhold forgiveness from those who will not forgive others. Perhaps you find yourself struggling with this truth as well. Let's take a moment to think through it together.

To fail to forgive others is a sin, and if we are walking in sin, how can we expect God to hear our prayers? Failing to forgive others shows that we have no comprehension of what we are really asking for, or of the magnitude of our own debt to a holy God. So many people want to skirt the truth of these verses. They either ignore them completely or attempt to explain them away somehow. Perhaps this is the reason for Jesus' words immediately following this model prayer. Without stopping for breath, He goes on to say in Matthew 6:14–15:

> "For if you forgive men for their transgressions, your heavenly Father will also forgive you. But if you do not forgive men, then your Father will not forgive your transgressions."

Why do you think people resist this truth?

Could it be that they want to come to God on their own terms? If so, we need to remember when we come to this point in prayer that we've already prayed, "Thy will be done, on earth as it is in heaven." If we have prayed this, then we should be ready to forgive our debtors, even as God forgives our debts.

And if we are still unwilling to forgive, if we refuse to obey in this matter, how can we expect a holy God to answer our prayers? Think about it, my friend.

Confession is the acknowledgment of our debt to God. Somewhere, somehow, you and I have failed to walk in righteousness, and when we fail, when we transgress the word and will of God, this must be acknowledged and forsaken.

The book of 1 John teaches us that if we are truly children of God, we will no longer live in habitual sin (1 John 3:6–10). Yes, we will commit singular acts of sin. That is why God gives us the assurance of 1 John 2:1–2:

> If anyone sins, we have an Advocate with the Father, Jesus Christ the righteous; and He Himself is the propitiation for our sins; and not for ours only, but also for *those of* the whole world.

The verb *sins* in 1 John 2:1 is in the aorist tense and implies a singular act of sin done at a point in time. Therefore, while a Christian cannot live in *habitual* sin, still a Christian can sin. Realizing this, God has made a wonderful provision for forgiveness in 1 John 1:9:

> If we confess our sins, He is faithful and righteous to forgive us our sins and to cleanse us from all unrighteousness.

Remember when I told you that I needed to go to Precept's video department and ask them to forgive me? Well, I did that, and they were sweet and loving, and forgave me. It's a wonderful feeling, Beloved, to be right with God and right with man. It's freeing! There is *nothing* like a clear conscience. The load is gone. You can breathe deeper, walk with a lighter step, and smile from the inside out. Why? Because you know there is nothing between you and God. You have done what is right, what pleases Him, and in doing so you have rolled the whole situation over onto His shoulders.

How I urge you, my friend, that if there is anything between you and God, or you and your fellow man, you settle it right away.

Keeping a clear conscience, a right relationship with God and others is to be a *daily* exercise. Just as we come before Him day by day, asking Him to supply our needs, we must also examine our hearts daily to see if we owe any debt of righteousness to God. If so, we need to confess it immediately.

Once you have confessed and forgiven, you come to the next index sentence.

"AND DO NOT LEAD US INTO TEMPTATION, BUT DELIVER US FROM EVIL."

This next index sentence is also a "stopper" which has thrown many people into a tailspin...but for a different reason.

People have asked me, "Kay, how can we say these words to God? Would God lead us into temptation?"

Obviously not. We need only to look at the words of James, who says:

Let no one say when he is tempted, "I am being tempted by God"; for God cannot be tempted by evil, and He Himself does not tempt anyone. But each one is tempted when he is carried away and enticed by his own lust. (James 1:13–14)

I call this sixth index sentence "preventative prayer" or "prayer for deliverance." I see it as the heart-cry of a child of God who longs for righteousness and yet is all too aware of the ever-present weakness of his flesh.

Remember when Jesus warned His disciples about sleeping in the

Garden of Gethsemane instead of keeping watch? Rather than catching up on their rest, they should have been praying, "Lord, my spirit is willing…but I know and understand the weakness of my flesh. And Lord, I'm crying to You to keep me from temptation and to deliver me from evil."

In light of this, I personally believe the sixth index sentence is a means of watching and praying so that you might not enter into temptation.

In the Old Testament, in another "model prayer," a godly man named Jabez prayed, "Oh that thou wouldest bless me indeed…and that thou wouldest keep *me* from evil, that it may not grieve me!" Scripture goes on to record that "God granted him that which he requested" (1 Chronicles 4:10, KJV).

It delights the heart of our Father when we cling to Him for holiness.

Well, Beloved, we have hurriedly come to that last index sentence:

"FOR THINE IS THE KINGDOM AND THE POWER,
AND THE GLORY, FOREVER. AMEN."

This brings us full circle in our prayer. We began with worship. We close with worship. The sentence begins with the word *for*. To me this suggests that all that has gone before is *because* of kingdom, *because* of His power, *because* of His eternal glory. And we, His children, the sheep of His pasture, the people of His hand, shout "Amen! So be it!"

For from Him and through Him and to Him are all things. To Him *be* the glory forever. Amen. (Romans 11:36)

Do you want to know how to pray? Is your heart's cry, "Lord, teach me to pray"?

Jesus says: "Pray, then, in this way.…"

DAY FOUR

Today we turn to that twice-repeated phrase in Matthew 6:16–18, "Whenever you fast…"

One of the first things you notice about this statement is that it seems to be a given with Jesus that God's children *will* fast. And who better than the Son of God Himself to tell us how and when and where to do it!

Let's pause at this point, then, examine the text, and see what we can learn on our own. As you read, mark every reference to *fast* or *fasting*.

➤ M A T T H E W   6 : 1 6 – 1 8

"And whenever you fast, do not put on a gloomy face as the hypocrites *do,* for they neglect their appearance in order to be seen fasting by men. Truly I say to you, they have their reward in full. But you, when you fast, anoint your head, and wash your face so that you may not be seen fasting by men, but by your Father who is in secret; and your Father who sees in secret will repay you."

Now list the main points this passage teaches regarding fasting.

As with other spiritual disciplines, we see once again that this action is directed toward our Father and has nothing to do with "putting on a show" for watching eyes. When we fast, we must not do anything that will draw attention to our appearance or our hunger or our dedication. Fasting is between an individual and his God.

Fasting implies abstinence. It usually refers to doing without food for a limited period of time. When you study what God's Word has to say about fasting, you will see that abstinence from food can be to various degrees and sometimes includes going without water.

So that you may be familiar with some of the passages on fasting, let me simply print out scriptures on the various types of fasting I have encountered in my study of God's Word. Read each one carefully. I would strongly suggest that you also look up and highlight these references in your own Bible. Next to each reference, write the word *fasting* in the margin of your Bible.

TYPES OF FASTING

1. PARTIAL:

In those days I, Daniel, had been mourning for three entire weeks. I did not eat any tasty food, nor did meat or wine enter my mouth, nor did I use any ointment at all, until the entire three weeks were completed. (Daniel 10:2–3)

2. TOTAL:

Then Jesus was led up by the Spirit into the wilderness to be tempted by the devil. And after He had fasted forty days and forty nights, He then became hungry. (Matthew 4:1–2)

3. ABSOLUTE (NO FOOD OR WATER):

"Go, assemble all the Jews who are found in Susa, and fast for me; do not eat or drink for three days, night or day. I and my maidens also will fast in the same way. And thus I will go in to the king, which is not according to the law; and if I perish, I perish." (Esther 4:16)

And he was three days without sight, and neither ate nor drank. (Acts 9:9)

4. VOLUNTARY (PURPOSELY TAKING NO FOOD):

So I gave my attention to the Lord God to seek *Him* by prayer and supplications, with fasting, sackcloth, and ashes. (Daniel 9:3)

5. INVOLUNTARY (CANNOT EAT) BECAUSE:

A. TOO GRIEVED, OR NO DESIRE:

Then the king went off to his palace and spent the night fasting, and no entertainment was brought before him; and his sleep fled from him. (Daniel 6:18)

B. NO FOOD AVAILABLE:

And Jesus called His disciples to Him, and said, "I feel compassion for the multitude, because they have remained with Me now for three days and have nothing to eat; and I do not wish to send them away hungry, lest they faint on the way." (Matthew 15:32)

But in everything commending ourselves as servants of God,…in beatings, in imprisonments, in tumults, in labors, in sleeplessness, in hunger. (2 Corinthians 6:4–5)

Why do people fast?

As you move through the Bible and examine each reference to fasting, you will see that people fasted for various reasons and in different ways. Sometimes individuals fasted, at other times people were called together or gathered for the sole purpose of fasting and seeking God .

Fasting can be sincere and for proper reasons. It can also be done for selfish purposes. The first is pleasing to God, the latter isn't. In Zechariah 7:5, God asks His people the question, "When you fasted and mourned in the fifth and seventh months these seventy years, was it actually for Me that you fasted?"

"Are you seeking Me," God asks, "or are you trying to manipulate Me?" It's a good question to ask ourselves when we fast. In Isaiah 58, God deals with the issue of manipulation. Take a few minutes to read Isaiah 58:1–12 and then answer the questions that follow. As you read the text, mark the words *fast* and *fasted*.

➤ I S A I A H   5 8 : 1 – 1 2

1 "Cry loudly, do not hold back;

Raise your voice like a trumpet,

And declare to My people their transgression,

And to the house of Jacob their sins.

2 "Yet they seek Me day by day, and delight to know My ways,

As a nation that has done righteousness,

And has not forsaken the ordinance of their God.

They ask Me *for* just decisions,

They delight in the nearness of God.

3 'Why have we fasted and Thou dost not see?

Why have we humbled ourselves and Thou dost not notice?'

Behold, on the day of your fast you find *your* desire,

And drive hard all your workers.

4 "Behold, you fast for contention and strife and to strike with a wicked
    fist.

You do not fast like *you do* today to make your voice heard on high.

5 "Is it a fast like this which I choose, a day for a man to humble himself?

Is it for bowing one's head like a reed,

And for spreading out sackcloth and ashes as a bed?

Will you call this a fast, even an acceptable day to the LORD?

6 "Is this not the fast which I chose,

To loosen the bonds of wickedness,

To undo the bands of the yoke,

And to let the oppressed go free,

And break every yoke?

7 "Is it not to divide your bread with the hungry,

And bring the homeless poor into the house;

When you see the naked, to cover him;

And not to hide yourself from your own flesh?

8 "Then your light will break out like the dawn,

And your recovery will speedily spring forth;

And your righteousness will go before you;

The glory of the LORD will be your rear guard.

9 "Then you will call, and the LORD will answer;

   You will cry, and He will say, 'Here I am.'

   If you remove the yoke from your midst,

   The pointing of the finger, and speaking wickedness,

10 And if you give yourself to the hungry,

   And satisfy the desire of the afflicted,

   Then your light will rise in the darkness,

   And your gloom *will become* like midday.

11 "And the LORD will continually guide you,

   And satisfy your desire in scorched places,

   And give strength to your bones;

   And you will be like a watered garden,

   And like a spring of water whose waters do not fail.

12 "And those from among you will rebuild the ancient ruins;

   You will raise up the age-old foundations;

   And you will be called the repairer of the breach,

   The restorer of the streets in which to dwell."

1. According to verses 1–4, why were they fasting?

2. Were they walking in righteousness before God?

3. Verse 5 tells you what they were doing when they fasted. List some of these things.

4. According to verses 6 and 7, what kind of fast had God chosen?

5. In verses 8–12 the words *then* and *if* appear several times in a very significant way. These show the end result of a godly fast. Read these verses, specifically looking for all the occurrences of *then* and *if*.

Fasting is usually born out of a need. Jesus brings this out in Matthew 9:14–15 when the disciples of John questioned Jesus' disciples because they were not fasting. Jesus replied by reminding them that the bridegroom was still with them and that when He was taken away, then they would fast. In essence, Jesus was saying, "I'm here, supplying their needs. Therefore, they don't need to fast. But when I'm gone, they will." When people fast, it is generally because they feel moved by a need! The needs can be quite varied, as we will see.

Fasting calls us from the preoccupations of body and soul in the day-by-day pressures of life. It summons us into such serious communion with our Lord that we voluntarily abstain from our normal absorption with such needs as food and drink. Could this be why more of us don't fast? Could it be that we're too busy? Too self-sufficient? Too self-absorbed?

Instead of seeking the Lord, we want to "try it ourselves first." Before we know it, we're over our heads in planning, scheming, and manipulating to bring about what we need and desire. If we're that busy, who has time for fasting? Fasting is for those who will put aside all else, including food, to seek God on some particular issue or need.

When, Beloved, was the last time you deemed something so important, so critical, that you sought God in prayer and fasting?

D A Y   F I V E

As I was on my way to Israel in 1994, I received a fax from Dr. Bill Bright, founder of Campus Crusade for Christ. He asked me to be part of a committee to invite other Christian leaders to join us in a time of fasting and prayer for revival in our nation. Bill had felt the leading of God to fast for forty days in the summer of 1994. It was in the middle of this fast that God laid this convocation on his heart. Out of this experience, he wrote the book *The Coming Revival: America's Call to Fast, Pray and "Seek God's Face."*

The following year I received another communication from Bill, asking me to be on the host committee as we sought to gather people from all over the United States to join us for three days of prayer and fasting. It was a monumental occasion as almost four thousand gathered daily to fast and intercede before the Father from nine in the morning until nine at night, without any breaks. We were gathered together as one (John 17) for one purpose — to confess our sins and beseech God to have mercy upon us and bring us to a genuine Word-based revival. Such holy convocations may be the last and only hope for our nation.

What will be the effect of it all? I have no idea. I only know that Dr. Bright and others of us are going to continue meeting like this until we pass the year 2000. While I do not know what effect such gatherings will have, I do know that what we are doing honors God. By fasting and praying together in such a way, we are saying that our eyes are on God alone, and that our only hope is in Him.

Now, in our final day of study this week, I want us to turn to the Word of God to see *when* people fasted. What occasions warranted fasting? The Scriptures give several illustrations.

Again let me print out various texts, and in the space provided underneath them, write down the occasion which prompted the fasting. Read each scripture carefully, then look it up in your Bible to put it into context.

Be sure to mark the text in your Bible so you will recognize it as a fasting passage.

WHEN DO PEOPLE FAST?

➤ 2 SAMUEL 1:12

And they mourned and wept and fasted until evening for Saul and his son Jonathan and for the people of the LORD and the house of Israel, because they had fallen by the sword.

➤ PSALM 35:13

But as for me, when they were sick, my clothing was sackcloth; I humbled my soul with fasting; And my prayer kept returning to my bosom.

➤ 2 SAMUEL 12:16, 21–23

David therefore inquired of God for the child; and David fasted and went and lay all night on the ground.... Then his servants said to him, "What is this thing that you have done? While the child was alive, you fasted and wept; but when the child died, you arose and ate food." And he said, "While the child was *still* alive, I fasted and wept; for I said, 'Who knows, the LORD may be gracious to me, that the child may live.' But now he has died; why should I fast? Can I bring him back again? I shall go to him, but he will not return to me."

➤ EZRA 8:21–23

Then I proclaimed a fast there at the river of Ahava, that we might humble ourselves before our God to seek from Him a safe journey for us, our little ones, and all our possessions. For I was ashamed to request from the king troops and horsemen to protect us from the enemy on the way, because we had said to the king, "The hand of our God is favorably disposed to all those who seek Him, but His power and His anger are against all those who forsake Him." So we fasted and sought our God concerning this *matter*, and He listened to our entreaty.

➤ J O N A H   3

Now the word of the LORD came to Jonah the second time, saying, "Arise, go to Nineveh the great city and proclaim to it the proclamation which I am going to tell you." So Jonah arose and went to Nineveh according to the word of the LORD. Now Nineveh was an exceedingly great city, a three days' walk. Then Jonah began to go through the city one day's walk; and he cried out and said, "Yet forty days and Nineveh will be overthrown." Then the people of Nineveh believed in God; and they called a fast and put on sackcloth from the greatest to the least of them. When the word reached the king of Nineveh, he arose from his throne, laid aside his robe from him, covered *himself* with sackcloth, and sat on the ashes. And he issued a proclamation and it said, "In Nineveh by the decree of the king and his nobles: Do not let man, beast, herd, or flock taste a thing. Do not let them eat or drink water. But both man and beast must be covered with sackcloth; and let men call on God earnestly that each may turn from his wicked way and from the violence which is in his hands. Who knows, God may turn and relent, and withdraw His burning anger so that we shall not perish?"

When God saw their deeds, that they turned from their wicked way, then God relented concerning the calamity which He had declared He would bring upon them. And He did not do *it*.

➤ J O E L   1 : 1 4 – 1 6 ;   2 : 1 – 2 ,   1 1 – 1 8

(You need to look up the context, as the first call to fasting was because of a plague of locusts, and the second was in light of the impending day of the Lord.)

Consecrate a fast,
Proclaim a solemn assembly;

Gather the elders
And all the inhabitants of the land
To the house of the LORD your God,
And cry out to the LORD.
Alas for the day!
For the day of the LORD is near,
And it will come as destruction from the Almighty.
Has not food been cut off before our eyes,
Gladness and joy from the house of our God?

Blow a trumpet in Zion,
And sound an alarm on My holy mountain!
Let all the inhabitants of the land tremble,
For the day of the LORD is coming;
Surely it is near,
A day of darkness and gloom,
A day of clouds and thick darkness.
As the dawn is spread over the mountains,
So there is a great and mighty people;
There has never been *anything* like it,
Nor will there be again after it
To the years of many generations....

And the LORD utters His voice before His army;
Surely His camp is very great,
For strong is he who carries out His word.
The day of the LORD is indeed great and very awesome,
And who can endure it?
"Yet even now," declares the LORD,
"Return to Me with all your heart,
And with fasting, weeping, and mourning;
And rend your heart and not your garments."
Now return to the LORD your God,
For He is gracious and compassionate,

Slow to anger, abounding in lovingkindness,
And relenting of evil.
Who knows whether He will *not* turn and relent,
And leave a blessing behind Him,
Even a grain offering and a libation
For the LORD your God?
Blow a trumpet in Zion,
Consecrate a fast, proclaim a solemn assembly,
Gather the people, sanctify the congregation,
Assemble the elders,
Gather the children and the nursing infants.
Let the bridegroom come out of his room
And the bride out of her *bridal* chamber.
Let the priests, the LORD's ministers,
Weep between the porch and the altar,
And let them say, "Spare Thy people, O LORD,
And do not make Thine inheritance a reproach,
A byword among the nations.
Why should they among the peoples say,
'Where is their God?'"

Then the LORD will be zealous for His land,
And will have pity on His people.

➤ ESTHER 3:13–4:17

And letters were sent by couriers to all the king's provinces to destroy, to kill, and to annihilate all the Jews, both young and old, women and children, in one day, the thirteenth *day* of the twelfth month, which is the month Adar, and to seize their possessions as plunder. A copy of the edict to be issued as law in every province was published to all the peoples so that they should be ready for this day. The couriers went out impelled by the king's command while the decree was issued in Susa the capital; and while the king and Haman sat down to drink, the city of Susa was in confusion.

When Mordecai learned all that had been done, he tore his clothes, put on sackcloth and ashes, and went out into the midst of the city and wailed loudly and bitterly. And he went as far as the king's gate, for no one was to enter the king's gate clothed in sackcloth. And in each and every province where the command and decree of the king came, there was great mourning among the Jews, with fasting, weeping, and wailing; and many lay on sackcloth and ashes.

Then Esther's maidens and her eunuchs came and told her, and the queen writhed in great anguish. And she sent garments to clothe Mordecai that he might remove his sackcloth from him, but he did not accept *them.* Then Esther summoned Hathach from the king's eunuchs, whom the king had appointed to attend her, and ordered him *to go* to Mordecai to learn what this *was* and why it *was.* So Hathach went out to Mordecai to the city square in front of the king's gate. And Mordecai told him all that had happened to him, and the exact amount of money that Haman had promised to pay to the king's treasuries for the destruction of the Jews. He also gave him a copy of the text of the edict which had been issued in Susa for their destruction, that he might show Esther and inform her, and to order her to go in to the king to implore his favor and to plead with him for her people.

And Hathach came back and related Mordecai's words to Esther. Then Esther spoke to Hathach and ordered him *to reply* to Mordecai: "All the king's servants and the people of the king's provinces know that for any man or woman who comes to the king to the inner court who is not summoned, he has but one law, that he be put to death, unless the king holds out to him the golden scepter so that he may live. And I have not been summoned to come to the king for these thirty days." And they related Esther's words to Mordecai.

Then Mordecai told *them* to reply to Esther, "Do not imagine that you in the king's palace can escape any more than all the Jews. For if you remain silent at this time, relief and deliverance will arise for the Jews from another place and you and your father's house will perish. And who knows whether you have not attained royalty for such a time as this?" Then Esther told *them* to reply to Mordecai, "Go, assemble all the Jews who are found in Susa, and fast for me; do not eat or drink for three days, night or day. I and my maidens also will fast in the same way. And thus I will go in to the king, which is not according to the law; and if I perish, I perish." So Mordecai went away and did just as Esther had commanded him.

➤ 1 KINGS 21:27–29

And it came about when Ahab heard these words, that he tore his clothes and put on sackcloth and fasted, and he lay in sackcloth and went about despondently. Then the word of the LORD came to Elijah the Tishbite, saying, "Do you see how Ahab has humbled himself before Me? Because he has humbled himself before Me, I will not bring the evil in his days, *but* I will bring the evil upon his house in his son's days."

➤ EZRA 10:6

Then Ezra rose from before the house of God and went into the chamber of Jehohanan the son of Eliashib. Although he went there, he did not eat bread, nor drink water, for he was mourning over the unfaithfulness of the exiles.

➤ ACTS 13:2–3

And while they were ministering to the Lord and fasting, the Holy Spirit said, "Set apart for Me Barnabas and Saul for the work to which I have called them." Then, when they had fasted and prayed and laid their hands on them, they sent them away.

➤ DANIEL 9:2-3

In the first year of his reign I, Daniel, observed in the books the number of the years which was *revealed as* the word of the LORD to Jeremiah the prophet for the completion of the desolations of Jerusalem, *namely,* seventy years. So I gave my attention to the Lord God to seek *Him by* prayer and supplications, with fasting, sackcloth, and ashes.

➤ LUKE 2:37

She never left the temple, serving night and day with fastings and prayers.

➤ 2 CORINTHIANS 6:4-5

...in everything commending ourselves as servants of God, in much endurance, in afflictions, in hardships, in distresses, in beatings, in imprisonments, in tumults, in labors, in sleeplessness, in hunger.

How I pray that you have taken the time to *carefully read* these passages. I really believe that God can use them to show you *when* you need to fast.

Aside from Isaiah 58 and Matthew 6, the Word of God doesn't really give a great deal of specific instruction regarding fasting. Only as we study various incidents of people's fasting do we gain more insights into the occasions that prompt people to seek Him in this way. Yesterday I said that fasting is usually born out of a need to diligently seek God. Isn't this what you saw as you looked up all those scriptures?

Let's take a look at some of them together, and briefly touch on what you might have seen. It will be good review and might touch a specific need in your own life, even as it has in mine. These passages have also been helpful to our staff as we meet once a month, taking one of our workdays for the purpose of prayer and fasting.

OCCASIONS FOR FASTING:

SORROW

Hannah's rival, Elkanah's second wife, provoked her mercilessly because of her barren womb. Hannah longed for children, but what could she do? The Lord had closed her womb. Year after year when they went to the temple to worship, her desolation and grief of spirit grew worse. Peninnah, Elkanah's second wife who had children, constantly and cruelly flaunted her privileged position as mother of Elkanah's children. Hannah's bitterness of soul was so great that she would not eat (1 Samuel 1:6–8). What a contrast to our thinking today. Instead of fasting for children, we abort them!

DEATH OF FRIENDS — OR ENEMIES

David and his men mourned and fasted until evening the day they heard of Saul's and Jonathan's deaths (2 Samuel 1:12). Torn by the malicious attacks of his enemy Saul, David nevertheless humbled his soul through fasting when he heard that this same enemy, along with David's friend Jonathan, had been killed. He mourned as if these two men had been members of his own family!

SERIOUS ILLNESS IN THE FAMILY

David fasted and stretched himself out on the ground to plead for the life of his child by Bathsheba. When the child died, David's fasting ended for the situation was resolved (2 Samuel 12:15–23).

SEEKING WISDOM AND GUIDANCE

Paul and Barnabas fasted and prayed before they appointed elders for the churches (Acts 14:23).

DESIRE FOR GOD'S HELP AND PROTECTION

Ezra proclaimed a fast at the river Ahava, that those traveling with him might humble themselves before God to seek from Him a safe journey through enemy territory. Rather than seeking the king's protection, he sought the Lord's glory through fasting and prayer, and God honored his faith (Ezra 8:21–23).

IN A DAY OF PENDING JUDGMENT

Times of God's judgment have also provoked people to fast — even ungodly people. This was the case in Nineveh when Jonah came pronouncing destruction because of the iniquity of Nineveh. From the king all the way down to the animals of Nineveh, none ate or drank. The whole nation was called to turn from their wickedness and to call upon God. As a result Nineveh was spared from destruction at that time. O that our nation would turn from its sin, fast, and pray! Surely this would bring revival to the church and salvation to multitudes in our nation.

In Joel, God calls to Israel, "Return to Me with all your heart, and with fasting, weeping, and mourning; and rend your heart and not your garments" (Joel 2:12–13). When I spoke briefly and then led a prayer at the recent Fasting and Prayer Convocation, this was one of the passages God led me to read to the assembly. I urged them to weep and mourn over all the abominations being committed in our land which grieve the great heart of God. And I do believe He moved in our midst during those days, as people heard the Word of God and truly sensed His heart and His passion.

O Beloved, read Ezekiel 9…and then consider a time of fasting and prayer where you might sigh and groan with the heart of God over all the abominations being committed in our land. Who knows? Perhaps the Lord has brought you, like Esther, to the kingdom for such a time as this!

A SIMPLE DESIRE TO SERVE GOD

This is so beautifully seen in the life of the prophetess Anna, who served God day and night in the temple with fastings and prayers (Luke 2:37).

ADDITIONAL REASONS TO FAST

The Bible gives us many additional reasons to fast. A deep desire for wisdom and a revelation of God's will led Daniel to turn aside from his routine and seek the Lord through fasting (Daniel 9:2–3). Ezra fasted and interceded out of mourning because of the unfaithfulness of the exiles who had returned to Jerusalem. In many manuscripts, Mark 9:29 and Matthew

17:21 indicate that certain kinds of demons only come out by prayer and fasting.

What about you, my friend? Would Jesus have an occasion to say to you, "When you fast..."?

When *do* you fast, Beloved? Do you see the need? Do you sense your Savior's passion and longing for lost men and women? How I pray that the Lord will stir you deep within to seek Him and to seek His will with all your heart.

CHAPTER SEVEN

THE DESIRE
FOR THINGS

D o not lay up for yourselves treasures upon earth, where moth and rust destroy, and where thieves break in and steal. But lay up for yourselves treasures in heaven, where neither moth nor rust destroys, and where thieves do not break in or steal; for where your treasure is, there will your heart be also" (Matthew 6:19–21).

Whenever I hear this verse, I can't help but remember the time Jack and I, as newlyweds, headed to Mexico as missionaries.

When we met and married, I was a widow with two children and a whole house full of furniture. Time and again I had told the Lord, "Father, I hold all this in an open hand. I want to serve You. It's Yours, and I am willing to walk out and leave it all whenever You ask me to."

Then came the test. Did I mean it?

We ran an ad in the newspaper that essentially said we were going to Mexico as missionaries and *everything* in our home was for sale. Although I can't remember what scripture we used twenty-nine years ago, I do recall including in the ad a biblical basis for "selling it all."

People converged upon our home, looking for bargains. And bargains they found. In the midst of strangers rummaging through my closets and cupboards a friend took me aside and said, "Kay, don't do this. Don't sell everything. Just put it in storage. Who knows, God may not let you stay in Mexico!"

Her words jarred me a little. The thought had never occurred to me. To

163

that point, leaving Mexico hadn't even entered my mind. Yet even as I paused to consider my friend's counsel, the words of Matthew 6:19 flooded my heart. "Do not lay up for yourselves treasures upon earth...."

The momentary doubt faded from my mind. Earthly treasures had to go. I could not go to Mexico with my heart in storage.

You know, Beloved, as I look back on those days, I have no regrets. Yes, in one way my friend had been right. God did not leave us in Mexico long-term. The heart condition that confined me to bed for a prolonged period of time and sent us back to the U.S.A. was part of God's sovereign design for our lives. He brought us home in order to establish Precept Ministries and eventually take us into ninety-three countries, with inductive Bible studies in more than twenty languages. When we left Mexico, however — since we couldn't see the future God had planned — I thought my heart would break. Truly the strings of my heart were entwined about the work God had given us in Guadalajara.

The possessions packed in that crude homemade trailer behind our station wagon meant very little to me compared to another treasure: the hearts of precious ones who had come to the Lord during our three and a half years in Mexico. Jesus Himself said:

> "Truly I say to you, there is no one who has left house or brothers or sisters or mother or father or children or farms, for My sake and for the gospel's sake, but that he shall receive a hundred times as much now in the present age, houses and brothers and sisters and mothers and children and farms, along with persecutions; and in the age to come, eternal life." (Mark 10:29–30)

Believe me, Jack and I had no thought at all of "giving in order to get," and yet upon our return from Mexico, God was pleased to give us back a hundredfold through generous friends who shared their homes, condominiums, food, clothing, and possessions. The open-handed giving of these dear friends has been a wonderful example for us as God has blessed us materially in the intervening years. It has been our heart-desire to give in the same way that others so selflessly gave to us.

Now, at age sixty-two, as I ready this manuscript for my publisher, I find myself really not wanting for anything materially. *And this is the very time when I need to exercise the most caution.* Scripture reminds us that having ample possessions can be a precarious spiritual position!

How wise Agur was to ask of God what he knew he needed:

> Keep deception and lies far from me,
> Give me neither poverty nor riches;
> Feed me with the food that is my portion,
> Lest I be full and deny *Thee* and say, "Who is the LORD?"
> Or lest I be in want and steal,
> And profane the name of my God.
> (Proverbs 30:8–9)

Could I ever find myself in a position of being full and denying my Lord? Could I ever allow the light within me to become darkness, as Jesus warned in the Sermon on the Mount? It's a danger for all of us, Beloved. The very blessings of the Lord can seduce our affections away from the Giver to the gifts...if we do not continue to hold them in an open hand.

As I have gone about holiday preparations in our home this year, getting ready for the arrival of family and friends, I have found my heart welling up with gratitude toward our Father. I'm so thankful for the beauty of our home and for its lovely and peaceful refuge (except for the phone). Yet as much as I enjoy and appreciate it, I have vowed not to allow it or the mundane affairs of life to keep me from venturing out to do His will. In this past calendar year alone, I have taught and ministered in twelve countries and been on the road for over six months. Why? Because this is what I felt the Lord would have me do at this stage in my life.

I know it may sound like a "glamorous adventure" to you, but those of us on the staff who travel would tell you otherwise. To us it is not a glamorous adventure but rather a privilege and an honor to represent Him wherever He sends us as His ambassadors. It is an act of obedience which we gladly perform. No, it is not without cost. But in the light of eternity and all its glory, those costs add up to nothing!

God says, "To whom much is given, much is required." As you travel abroad, you begin to realize just how much God has lavished on the United States of America in both material and spiritual blessings. We have more freedom than others, more access to the media, more Bibles in all varieties, more literature, more schools, more training, more churches, more missions, more numbers of professing believers, more...more...more.

We have sung it over and over again: "God Bless America." And He has. I don't imagine that any other nation on the face of this earth has been as blessed as America. Yet what has happened to us? In our prosperity we have turned from God. We have forgotten that no one can serve two masters and that our affections cannot be divided. God knows this, and that is why He says either we will hate the one and love the other, or we will hold to the one and despise the other. We cannot serve God and riches.

Could this be a big reason why America has turned its back upon God? Is this why so many Americans who profess to know Him simply give Him lip service? Might this be why so many reflect the lukewarm attitude of the church at Laodicea, which said, "I am rich, and have become wealthy, and have need of nothing"? Do we, like they, fail to realize that we are "wretched and miserable and poor and blind and naked" (Revelation 3:17)?

Have our hearts become captivated with the seductiveness of "things" rather than with a fervent sacrificial love for our God and for the furtherance of His kingdom?

Statistics show us that evangelical Christians spend more for cat and dog food than they do for missions. It's alarming, isn't it? But what I'm about to tell you is, to me, more startling. People who make fifty thousand dollars or more annually give an average of 1 to 2 percent of their income to the church. People earning ten thousand dollars or less per year give an average of 10 to 20 percent of their income to the church.

These statistics sound like warning shots to my ear. It seems that the more we can accumulate "things," the more vulnerable we become to having our hearts enticed away from a sacrificial love for our God. Once money becomes our intimate companion and we no longer have to scrimp and save, we seem to spend it with greater ease. Finally we find ourselves squeezed in the vise of self-indulgence.

In Matthew 6:19, Jesus begins a series of "do not's." The first says, "Do not lay up...treasure on earth." The second is "Do not be anxious for your life...nor for your body." We will look closely at these "do not's" this week. Before we do, however, would you begin your study with me by asking God to reveal to you where your treasures are and what causes you to be anxious?

Are you willing to tell Him you will walk in obedience to what He shows you, even if it's difficult?

Will you ask Him to help you evaluate the ways you expend your energies, to show you if you are being wise in redeeming the time and making it count for eternity?

Would you ask Him to give you a glimpse of the treasures you can have in heaven?

I would not ask you to do this alone, Beloved. I will do it with you, because God would not honor my efforts if I were unwilling to let Him work in me as He works in you.

Now then, let's begin our week by reading Matthew 6:19–34 in the back of this book. This will put us into the context of what we want to study this week. As you read this passage, mark or underline every reference to the "listeners" in a distinctive color. This means you will mark every *you, your,* and *yourselves.* Then, when you finish, make a list of everything you observe from the text as a result of marking each reference.

Record that list below and on the next page. It may seem tedious, but I promise you that if you will think about all you are recording, it will be a powerful assignment. Don't procrastinate — do it now or you may miss what God wants to say to your heart.

OBSERVATIONS FROM THE TEXT

What do you and I really treasure? Whose opinion counts most with us — God's, or our neighbors' and friends'? What do we care most about — the applause of the world or the approval of God? Are we in danger of becoming entangled with the affairs of this life, forgetting that we are soldiers on active duty?

Look at the list you made today; read again what God says to you. How do you measure up? Do you believe what He says? Do you live accordingly?

Get on your knees, Beloved. I mean literally get on your knees and read through Matthew 6:19–34 again. As you do, ask God to cleanse you through the washing of the water of His Word. Ask Him to reveal to you any area of life where you might be in danger, or veering off track. Then record below what comes to your heart. You might want to write out a prayer…a poem…or a statement of faith.

DAY   TWO

How do you keep from laying up treasures on earth? Or to put it another way, how do you handle the seductiveness of things that would consume your energies and draw you away from undistracted devotion to your God? It's something we all need to know, isn't it?

I think we can find Jesus' answer to that question in Matthew 6:22–23:

"The lamp of the body is the eye; if therefore your eye is clear [healthy], your whole body will be full of light. But if your eye is bad, your whole body will be full of darkness. If therefore the light that is in you is darkness, how great is the darkness!"

The problem is our eyes; they're the path of seduction. It's a problem as old as the Garden of Eden, as old as the moment Satan enticed Eve. Eve's downfall came when she took her focus off God and put it upon the fruit of the tree of the knowledge of good and evil.

> When the woman saw that the tree was good for food, and that it was a delight to the eyes, and that the tree was desirable to make *one* wise, she took from its fruit and ate; and she gave also to her husband with her, and he ate. (Genesis 3:6)

Do you see the progression in this verse? First, Eve *saw,* and what she saw was desirable; so she took it, ate it, and then gave it to her husband. She saw, desired, took, ate...and gave it to another.

We see that same pattern in the book of Joshua. When God gave Jericho to the people of Israel, He clearly warned them that the city was under His ban and that all the possessions of that city belonged to Him. They were not allowed to take any spoils of war. God had said, "But as for you, only keep yourselves from the things under the ban, lest you covet *them* and take some of the things under the ban, so you would make the camp of Israel accursed and bring trouble on it" (Joshua 6:18).

The word of God was very clear. You could not miss what God was saying, yet one man named Achan did not heed God's warning. As a result, trouble indeed came to Israel. As a matter of fact, Israel's warriors became so powerless they could not even conquer the tiny town of Ai. God was not with them because there was sin in the camp. When they finally discovered that Achan's transgression was the cause of their defeat, he told the tragic story of his downfall:

> "When I saw among the spoil a beautiful mantle from Shinar and two hundred shekels of silver and a bar of gold fifty shekels in weight, then I coveted them and took them; and behold, they are concealed in the earth inside my tent with the silver underneath it." (Joshua 7:21)

Once again you see a pattern similar to Eve's. Achan *saw* the spoil, coveted or desired it, and then he took it. His downfall began with the focus of his eyes.

The same problem and the same pattern are evident in David's life as recorded in 2 Samuel 11. From his rooftop David *saw* a beautiful woman bathing, and he desired her. So he sent a messenger to inquire about her, and finally he took her. In all three incidents we have a pattern that moves from seeing, to desiring, to taking. As a consequence, others are affected. No matter what we may think, we never sin in isolation. Our sins hurt more than ourselves!

When you consider these things, is it any wonder Jesus tells us that the lamp of the body is the eye? Close your eyes for a moment. What do you see? Darkness. Nothing. Our eyes are the windows that let light into our bodies. Clean windows let in more light. Dirty windows obscure the light. Our eyes, therefore, determine the amount of light that comes into our bodies.

My dear Grandma Elsie died at the age of one hundred. In her later years she was afflicted with glaucoma. Her eyes were unhealthy. They didn't adjust well to changes in lighting, couldn't distinguish colors well, and suffered from blurred vision. It affected virtually everything she did. Our greatest concern, of course, was that she would stumble and fall.

What was physically true of Grandma Elsie is spiritually true of many Christians. Their eyes are not healthy. Their focus is on the wrong things. Because of that, their whole body is full of darkness. Consequently they stumble through life, groping along the way because they cannot see clearly.

In John's first letter he warned us about the lust of our eyes.

For all that is in the world, the lust of the flesh and the lust of the eyes and the boastful pride of life, is not from the Father, but is from the world. (1 John 2:16)

Because our eyes can be an instrument of lust — because they can lead us into the sin of covetousness — it is vital that we keep our eyes healthy. But how? We live in a world filled with all sorts of alluring things. Beautiful. Enticing. Pleasing. But so very distracting! Books, magazines, television, movies, billboards, and now even computers constantly display treasures belonging to this life and this life only. How then can a child of God keep his vision clear?

Focus!

As the author of Hebrews says, we need to fix our eyes on Jesus, the author and perfecter of our faith. Or as Paul says in 2 Corinthians 4:18, we need to look "not at the things which are seen, but at the things which are not seen, for the things which are seen are temporal, but the things which are not seen are eternal." We need to do as Moses did when he deliberately turned his back on Egypt and its treasures, "choosing rather to endure ill-treatment with the people of God, than to enjoy the passing pleasures of sin; considering the reproach of Christ greater riches than the treasures of Egypt; for he was looking to the reward. By faith he left Egypt, not fearing the wrath of the king; for he endured, as seeing Him who is unseen" (Hebrews 11:25–27).

It's all a matter of perspective, Beloved. Eternal perspective. Where is your focus? Is it upon the things of this world? Is it riveted to the treasures of this life that can be consumed by moths and rust and stolen by thieves? Or is it upon heavenly treasures that have eternal value?

The more comfortable we become, the more we acquire, the more we attain, the harder it becomes for us to remember that we are only "strangers and pilgrims" upon this earth and that "our citizenship is in heaven, from which also we eagerly wait for a Savior, the Lord Jesus Christ" (Philippians 3:20).

Someday everything on earth is going to burn, destroyed with an intense heat. Every record of human accomplishment, every impressive monument, everything that can be made with human hands will be dissolved by fire (2 Peter 3:10–12). Only that which was done by the Spirit of God, through channels of human flesh, will abide. These will become our treasures in heaven — the things that we have done by the Spirit in accordance with the Word of God and for God's glory.

Oh that we would see this, Beloved. O that the eyes of our understanding would be open so that we would not give our time and energies to those things which would only bring us passing earthly treasures.

I must ask you, my friend, what is your focus? Upon what have you set your heart and affections? Where are your treasures? How clear, how healthy are your eyes?

Take a few minutes and think about what distracts you from pure devotion to Jesus Christ. Then ask yourself what you need to do about it…and what the danger might be if you do nothing. Record your response below.

DAY THREE

When we do not fix our eyes upon Jesus and things of eternity, we will eventually find ourselves no longer serving God, but serving material possessions.

"Oh no, Kay," you might reply. "Not me! I have them both in proper perspective."

Are you sure?

I remember a time when a friend of mine happened into a small convenience store. The magazines on the rack in that store were so perverted and distressing my friend felt compelled to speak to the store owner. As she did, she confessed Jesus Christ as her Savior.

The man replied, "I'm a Christian also, ma'am, but God is God and business is business."

Is that true? Can God be kept in a Sunday box, served and worshiped one or two days out of the week while we devote the other days to "business"? Can we serve two masters? Jesus says no. "No one can serve two masters; for either he will hate the one and love the other, or he will hold to one and despise the other. You cannot serve God and mammon" (Matthew 6:24).

What did Jesus mean by the word *mammon*? James Boice, in his book *The Sermon on the Mount* explains it well:

Mammon was a word for material possessions, but it had come into Hebrew from a root word meaning "to entrust," or "to place in someone's keeping." Mammon therefore meant the wealth that one entrusted to another for safekeeping. At this time the word did not have any bad connotations at all and a rabbi could say, "Let the mammon of thy neighbor be as dear to thee as thine own." As time passed, however, the sense of the word mammon shifted away from the passive sense of "that which is entrusted" to the active sense of "that in which a man trusts." In this case, of course, the meaning was entirely bad, and the word mammon which was originally spelled with a small "m" came to be spelled with a capital "M" as designating a god. This linguistic development repeats itself in the life of anyone who does not have his eyes fixed on spiritual treasures. Is that true of you? Have things become your God? Don't forget that these things are written to Christians, and that they are therefore meant to make you ask whether the Lord God Almighty occupies the central place in your life or whether things obscure him.[1]

Dwight Pentecost adds these insights:

Mammon is the personalization of God's chief rival — money or material things. Our Lord viewed the acquisition of wealth as a goal that brings a man into the most abject slavery, that prevents him from discharging his responsibilities as one enslaved to Jesus Christ. He becomes enslaved instead to money and can serve no one else, least of all God. When a man is consumed by a passion to accumulate material things, there is room for no other love. The Lord did not condemn possession of wealth. He did condemn being possessed by that wealth. He viewed the love of money as gross idolatry.[2]

What is God's chief rival in our society today?

I believe it is "things." The god called "Mammon." Material possessions.

I'm reluctant to use the word "riches" here because you might reply in your mind, "But I'm not rich! I just want enough to get by on. All I want are the necessities of life. That can't be wrong, can it?" Yes, it can be wrong… if you are anxious about them…or if your necessity list doesn't match God's! This is why in the very next verse in Matthew 6 Jesus goes on to talk about being anxious — anxious over life's daily necessities. After all, if the necessities are taken care of, then what is there to be anxious about?

Read through Matthew 6:19–34 again in the back of your book. This time as you read, mark in a distinctive color or way every occurrence of the word *anxious*. Also mark every reference to *masters* along with any pronouns. Then when you finish, look at each occurrence of *anxious* in the text and record below what God says about being anxious.

Now then, Beloved, let's ask and answer some questions:

Are you serving God, or are you serving things? Why? You cannot serve both. Listen to Paul's perspective:

> I count all things to be loss in view of the surpassing value of knowing Christ Jesus my Lord, for whom I have suffered the loss of all things, and count them but rubbish in order that I may gain Christ. (Philippians 3:8)

Paul's eyes were fixed on the prize of the upward call of God in Christ Jesus. He served One and One alone, his Lord Jesus Christ. Consequently he tells us that he learned to be content in whatever circumstances he found himself. That word *learned* is important. It was an acquired skill! He *learned* how to get along with humble means and how to live in prosperity. In any and every circumstance of life he *learned* the secret of being filled and of going hungry, of having abundance and suffering need (Philippians 4:11–12). Paul would not permit anything to matter to him except that which had eternal value. Now that is something to learn, isn't it?

O Beloved, what about you? Where are you? To what are you giving yourself, your energies? Whom are you serving? What do you desire above all else and more than anything else in this life? What is your heart fixed upon? Is it upon God...or the temporal things of unrighteous mammon? What possesses you? Is it a passion for God...or a passion for the toys and tinsel of this life? Ponder these questions. Let them search your heart. Give God time to speak.

DAY   FOUR

"All I want are the necessities of life! I'm not interested in being rich, I just want to *survive!* Is anything wrong with that?"

It all depends on how you intend to survive. If surviving means that you do not have time to seek God's kingdom and God's righteousness, then you are not serving God, but mammon. And God says that is wrong.

Once again I want you to turn to the Sermon on the Mount in the back of this book and read through Matthew 6:19–34. Remember, reading the passage aloud will always help you remember it better. Our eyes have a natural tendency to skim when we are reading, but you can't do that if you are pronouncing each word! This time as you read, mark every reference to God in this passage. Note how Jesus refers to Him. Then when you finish, list below everything you learn from this text about God.

Have you forgotten, Beloved, that you have a heavenly Father and that it is His responsibility to take care of His children? How I love the fact that in this sermon Jesus keeps referring to God as our heavenly Father. It is not by accident, but by design. Fathers are expected to give their children the basics of life, to provide them with food and clothing. Isn't this what you saw earlier when we studied "The Lord's Prayer"? *Our Father...give us this day our daily bread.* God will always be the parent; you will always be His child. Since you are a child of God, it is God's responsibility as your Father to take care of the necessities of your life. It is your responsibility as a child of God to seek first His kingdom and His righteousness. Test Him...try Him with faith.

Let me tell you a story, Beloved, that vividly illustrates the truth of Matthew 6:25–33. Years ago when Russia was still under communism, God burdened me along with countless others to pray for the body of Jesus Christ living behind the Iron Curtain. Several publications from different organizations gave us plenty of fuel for prayer, one of which was called *A Bible for Russia.*

In the December 1983 issue of this periodical, I came across a story entitled "Christmas Eve in Romania." When I finished reading it, all I could do was weep and worship my God. Let me share the story with you, that you might weep, worship, and have your faith strengthened.

Christmas was not to be the same this year.

Isolated from the rest of the outside world, it was difficult with the seven children to celebrate the birth of Jesus, when their stomachs were empty. There were no decorations, no brightly lit candles, no Christmas tree, no cookies, and no beautiful wrapped gifts to exchange. The children were just as hungry today as any other day. Soon, Dad would be telling the children about the Messiah, born in a manger, much like the little hut they lived in.

This father, mother, and their seven children all under 14 years of age, were banished into exile in the far reaches of an uninhabited part of the country. The communist authorities hated the father because of his convicting preaching. He was nicknamed by the believers, "The Golden Word," because of his eloquence. They were forced to move to a little village, inaccessible by car or train. What food they were given was flown in by helicopter. They lived in a tiny hut with a straw roof, under the constant surveillance of the prison guards.

The village was established for those "undesirables" of society, which includes "religious fanatics." The stinging chill was made worse by the wind whipping snow across the flat barren land, unbroken by hills, and whistling its song through every crack and crevice in the small hut. For two days, the guards had not bothered to bring them any food. They were too busy preparing their own celebration with wine and pork. The children listened intently to their father telling them the story of Jesus, huddled together around the dim light of the gas lantern on the table. They were so intent they forgot about their hunger. But when the story was over, one after the other began to cry.

Before going to bed that Christmas Eve, the whole family knelt down on the dirt floor and prayed as never before: "Our Father, which art in heaven…give us this day our daily bread…."

After they finished their prayer and said, "Amen," the children asked their mother and father many questions.

"Do you think God heard our prayer?"

"Of course He did."

"But what if He didn't hear it?"

"That isn't possible," the father replied.

"Do you think He will send us bread?" they asked.

"Yes, I'm sure He will," said the father.

"But when?" they cried.

The parents, heartbroken to see their children crying from hunger, could not answer. The children continued to ask:

"Who will He send to bring us bread?"

"He will find someone," said the father.

"But what if He doesn't find anyone?"

"Well then…" the father paused, "He Himself will bring it with His own hand. Now close your eyes and go to sleep."

The father blew out the little lantern as darkness descended on them, and the wind whistled to them in their sleep. Suddenly, the still darkness was shattered, a knock on the door!

The father got out of bed, and opened the door just a crack to keep the cold from blowing inside. A hand holding a large loaf of bread was stretched toward him. His heart pounding, the father reached out to take the bread, and at the same time opened the door widely to say thank you. But at that very moment, in the twinkling of an eye, the hand was gone. There was no one there. Bewildered, the father closed the door and turned around. All seven children leaped out of bed and surrounded him.

"Who was it, Dad? Who gave you the bread?"

"Children," he said with a tremble in his voice, "the Lord did not find anyone to send to us with bread, so He Himself came and gave it to us with His own hand."

Nobody could sleep anymore that Christmas Eve. The children couldn't stop singing about Jesus, and about how the Lord had spread a table for them in the wilderness.[3]

O Beloved, we can serve God, and in serving God we need not be anxious about our lives or our bodies. Why? Because we are God's children, and He promises to supply all of our needs according to His riches in glory through Christ Jesus our Lord (Philippians 4:19). Your responsibility is simply to seek first His kingdom and His righteousness and know that in doing so all these things shall be added unto you.

DAY FIVE

Does seeking the kingdom of God and His righteousness liberate a man or a woman from all responsibility for earning a living? Is Matthew 6:33 a license for laziness or an undisciplined life? Does it mean that all I need to do is sit, pray, study, and meditate — and expect God to feed and clothe me?

Some think so, but their thinking isn't based on the whole counsel of God. That is why, my friend, I want to commend you for studying God's Word in such a way that you deal with scriptures within their *context,* in order to gain a more accurate understanding.

Every now and then we have people who come through our Precept Ministries campus, "moving according to the Spirit's leading." They have no jobs. They have no money. They simply go "wherever the Spirit leads them."

As they go, however, whose food do they eat? Others not only had to earn the money to buy it but also expend themselves to cook it.

And who pays the electric bill so they might sleep in a warm room? Who pays the water bill so they will have water with which to bathe and wash their clothes? And who invested the efforts to wash the sheets so that their bedding might be clean and crisp?

Someone had to do all these things. Someone had to invest time, resources, or labor.

What then are these wandering ones doing? They say they are seeking God's kingdom and righteousness. But what does God say? Is Matthew 6:33 a license for an undisciplined life? Does it set us free from the responsibility of earning a living?

These are questions we must answer so that we don't go off on seemingly "spiritual" but unbiblical tangents.

Second Thessalonians 3:6–15 speaks to this issue, so let's read it and then see what we can learn by answering some questions on the text. As you read, please note that the word *unruly* (3:6) may also legitimately be translated *undisciplined*. As you read the text, mark in distinctive ways the following key words: *undisciplined, example, and work (or working)*.

➤ 2 THESSALONIANS 3:6–15

6 Now we command you, brethren, in the name of our Lord Jesus Christ, that you keep aloof from every brother who leads an unruly life and not according to the tradition which you received from us.

7 For you yourselves know how you ought to follow our example, because we did not act in an undisciplined manner among you,

8 nor did we eat anyone's bread without paying for it, but with labor and hardship we *kept* working night and day so that we might not be a burden to any of you;

9 not because we do not have the right *to this*, but in order to offer ourselves as a model for you, that you might follow our example.

10 For even when we were with you, we used to give you this order: if anyone will not work, neither let him eat.

11 For we hear that some among you are leading an undisciplined life, doing no work at all, but acting like busybodies.

12 Now such persons we command and exhort in the Lord Jesus Christ to work in quiet fashion and eat their own bread.

13 But as for you, brethren, do not grow weary of doing good.

14 And if anyone does not obey our instruction in this letter, take special note of that man and do not associate with him, so that he may be put to shame.

15 And *yet* do not regard him as an enemy, but admonish him as a brother.

1. According to this passage, what is an undisciplined manner of life? (When you answer this, don't forget to note what verse 8 says.)

2. What example did Paul and his companions set before others? List everything you observe about their example.

3. What was Paul's order or command in verse ten?

4. Now according to what you have seen in 2 Thessalonians 3, does Matthew 6:33 say that we do not have to work to earn a living?

I think it's obvious from the text that Matthew 6:33 is not a license for an undisciplined life. Rather, Jesus combines a command and a promise. The command is that we are to habitually seek first God's kingdom and His righteousness. I say habitually because the verb *seek* is in the present tense in the Greek, which implies continuous or habitual action.

The word I really want you to notice is the word *first*. In all things God is to have the preeminence. The priority of our lives is to be His righteousness. God is not saying that you and I cannot do anything else. He knows that we live in the world and that we have responsibilities. Men are responsible to provide for their households. If they do not, Scripture says they are worse than infidels. A married woman is to be a keeper of her home, according to Scripture. The home is her responsibility. If she fails in keeping a proper home, then she has failed in what God has ordained for her to do. Providing for a family, keeping a home, or taking care of children requires huge amounts of time and energy. Any one of these tasks can be exhausting. (And trying to do all three defies description!)

These things cannot be neglected — nor does God expect us to neglect them for His kingdom. He does, however, expect us to keep them in proper perspective to the kingdom. *Our love, devotion, and obedience for Him are to supersede all else.* And when it does, we have the blessed promise: "All these things shall be added to you."

Let me repeat it once more. There is a command: "Seek first His kingdom and His righteousness." And there is a promise: "All these things shall be added to you."

What then, Beloved, is the bottom line of it all? Jesus said it, but let me repeat it: *Do not be anxious for tomorrow.*

How I love that statement "for tomorrow." Why doesn't it say don't be anxious for today? Because today, you are all right. It's not today that we normally worry about. Today you have something to put on your body.

Today you have something, however meager it may be, to put in your mouth. But you may say, "What about tomorrow?" God says tomorrow will care for itself. Why? Because God is not only a God of today, but a God of tomorrow. Each day has enough trouble of its own. We are to live one day at a time. That's why Jesus taught us to pray, "Give us this day our daily bread." If He took care of you today, will He not take care of you tomorrow?

Look at those little birds out there. Aren't you worth more than they? Of course you are. Your heavenly Father feeds them and He'll feed you also.

And why are you anxious about clothing? Observe how the lilies of the field grow; they do not toil nor do they spin, yet I say to you that even Solomon in all his glory did not clothe himself like one of these. But if God so arrays the grass of the field, which is alive today and tomorrow is thrown into the furnace, *will He* not much more *do so for* you, O men of little faith? (Matthew 6:28–30)

Tell me, Beloved, just what kind of Father do you have? Is He faithless or faithful? Can He lie?

Of course He cannot lie. And yes, He is always faithful. As Paul wrote to Timothy, "If we are faithless, He remains faithful; for He cannot deny Himself" (2 Timothy 2:13). You can trust Him, so quit being anxious! It's so unnecessary. It's also a sin. It is an accusation against the very faithfulness of God.

Are you poor? Then listen to God's Word.

Godliness *actually* is a means of great gain, when accompanied by contentment. For we have brought nothing into the world, so we cannot take anything out of it either. And if we have food and covering, with these we shall be content. (1 Timothy 6:6–8)

Are you rich? Then listen to God's instructions.

Instruct those who are rich in this present world not to be conceited or to fix their hope on the uncertainty of riches, but on God, who richly supplies us with all things to enjoy. *Instruct them* to do good, to be rich in good works, to be generous and ready to share, storing up for themselves the treasure of a good foundation for the future, so that they may take hold of that which is life indeed. (1 Timothy 6:17–19)

Rich or poor, set your affection on things above (Colossians 3:2). Seek first His kingdom and His righteousness and know, beloved child of God, that all these things will be added to you.

We have His word on it.

CHAPTER EIGHT

TO JUDGE
OR NOT
TO JUDGE

DAY ONE

Even if my friend *is* living in sin, if she tells me she's saved, then who am I to question her salvation? The Bible tells me not to judge her! The Bible says that if we accept Jesus into our hearts, then we're saved no matter what we do."

The young college student standing before me was earnest, adamant, and charming. I loved talking to her. But was she right in her understanding of the Bible?

How many times have you heard someone quote, "Judge not, that ye be not judged"?

How many times have you called sinful behavior into question and been told (with a self-righteous flutter of the eyelids), "Judge not, that ye be not judged"?

Or have you ever mentioned to another that you were concerned about a person's salvation only to hear, "Who are we to judge? Don't you know the Bible says, 'Judge not'?"

To be honest, at times I've thought that's the only verse of the Bible some people can quote. It's always intended to stop a conversation in its tracks, shift the subject, and outweigh any other biblical evidence. After all, it's one part of Scripture which lets people off the proverbial hook! Or so they think!

In one form or another, most of us have heard the debates over this well-known phrase, haven't we? Does the Bible actually say, "Judge not, that ye be not judged"? Yes, it does. In good old King James English, that's exactly what it says in Matthew 7:1. The only problem is, so many who quote Matthew 7:1 rip it totally out of context. They forget or ignore the four verses which *follow* Matthew 7:1 — verses which explain just what Jesus meant when He spoke to His disciples on this matter of judging.

Is all judging wrong? This is our topic of study for the week, and I promise you, Beloved, if you will "hangeth thou in there" and study well, I think you will know exactly what this verse means and how to apply it to your life. Not because you will have learned my interpretation of it, but because you will have examined it for yourself, first in its immediate context and then in the context of the broader teaching of the Word of God.

Now, let's get started. As a first step in the process, take a few minutes to read Matthew 6:19–7:28 in your Bible or in the back of this book so that you can put Matthew 7:1 in its immediate context. When you finish reading, list below the main topics that are covered in these verses, beginning with 6:19 and moving through 7:28.

Remember, we are in a succession of "do not's" at this point in our study of the Sermon of the Mount. Jesus has already said:
- "Do not lay up for yourselves treasures."
- "Do not be anxious for your life...nor for your body."
- "Do not be anxious for tomorrow."

Three more "do not's" follow:
- "Do not judge."
- "Do not give what is holy to dogs."
- "Do not throw your pearls before swine."

If you stop and think about it, the last three seem incongruous. One says not to judge, and the other two say not to give what is holy to dogs nor to throw pearls before swine. If you don't judge, how are you going to know who are dogs and who are swine?

In the same chapter Jesus also tells us that we will know false prophets by their fruits. If I'm not allowed to judge, then how am I going to "inspect their fruit" so I'll know which prophets are false?

Do all these questions create problems? What is the context of this "judge not" verse really saying to us?

Matthew 7:1–5 is printed out for your convenience. Read it carefully, and as you do, mark every occurrence of the word *judge*. By the way, the word for *judge* is *krino* in the Greek. It means to assume the office of a judge, to condemn, to give sentence, to undergo the process of a trial, or to execute judgment upon.

➤ MATTHEW 7:1–5

1 "Do not judge lest you be judged.

2 "For in the way you judge, you will be judged; and by your standard of measure, it will be measured to you.

3 "And why do you look at the speck that is in your brother's eye, but do not notice the log that is in your own eye?

4 "Or how can you say to your brother, 'Let me take the speck out of your eye,' and behold, the log is in your own eye?

5 "You hypocrite, first take the log out of your own eye, and then you will see clearly to take the speck out of your brother's eye."

Now then, let's clarify our understanding of this text by answering the following questions. As you answer them, record what you learn from simply observing the text itself.

1. According to this passage, there's a problem with your brother's eye and your own eye. Note below what is in your brother's eye and what's in your eye.

2. Does this passage actually forbid you to take the speck out of your brother's eye?

3. What conditions does the passage list for this speck removal?

4. What is Jesus' warning in verse 2? Put it in your own words.

5. What does Jesus call the person who tries to take the speck out of his brother's eye without first taking care of his own eye? Why do you think He calls him that?

6. Do you think this passage forbids judging…or just a certain kind of judging? Explain your answer.

To understand what God is saying to us in this passage, we need to look at three "whats" on judging.
- What is the context and the content of this passage?
- What makes this judging wrong?
- What am I to judge, if anything?

We'll examine these three "whats" thoroughly over the next few days.

D A Y   T W O

When our youngest son, David, was still at home, our refrigerator had a little sticker on it that read, "Christians aren't perfect, just forgiven."

For a teenager whose father was the president of a Christian organization and whose mother was a Bible teacher and conference speaker, it was a comforting reminder. It was an especially needed motto when you consider that the public seems to expect an elevated standard of behavior from children of such parents — a standard they often don't hold even for their own children!

There was another slogan floating around during that same era. Many Christians were wearing a little button on their lapel that read: PBPGIN-FWMY. Do you remember that? Do you remember its translation? *Please Be Patient. God Is Not Finished With Me Yet!*

That's what we want, isn't it? Patience for our imperfections! Not tolerance of sin, but a little grace and patience while we grow (ever so slowly) into the image of our Lord Jesus Christ. We long for that grace and patience. We delight in it, welcoming it with open arms. We want those friends who will love and understand us, warts and all. Yet…is that what we give others?

Read Matthew 7:1–5 again before you go any further. Then answer this question: What makes the "judgment" in this passage wrong?

You know the judgment that Jesus forbids in Matthew 7 is wrong because Jesus refers to those who judge this way as hypocrites. They are hypocrites because they concern themselves with a speck in their brother's eye even while they are stumbling around with beams under their own eyelids! They expect perfection from others but are far from perfect themselves. They have an attitude that can only be described as "judgmental."

Did you notice the blatant contrast in those verses? A beam versus a mote! A log compared to a speck! Quite a contrast, isn't it? And remember, Scripture says we will be judged according to the way we judge! The standard of measure we use will be the measure by which we are measured! That's a sobering thought. Do I expect the same thing from myself that I consistently expect from others? Am I willing to give the kind of mercy I would like to receive? Am I willing to extend the sort of love that grants grace and covers imperfections?

The judging that Jesus calls hypocritical is that which notices specks in the eyes of others and misses the logs and beams so near at hand. And let me tell you, Beloved, those who employ this kind of judging can be unbelievably destructive.

People in public ministry are especially subject to criticism. Our blunders in this day and age are often recorded on cassette tapes, reproduced quickly, and projected across the country. The world of video and television has not only left us open to criticism for what we say but also for the way we look, dress, or act. Every slip of the tongue or peculiar mannerism is recorded for the world to see. Obviously anyone in this position becomes extremely vulnerable, open to criticism from all sides.

Yes, there is certainly a place for constructive criticism. All criticism is not judgmental. Many times I have received precious letters born out of hearts of loving concern for the work of the Lord and for me. When I read a letter like that, I realize that my friends have been careful to remove the log out of their own eyes before sitting down to write me. I know they are seeing clearly, for their surgery is done with extreme gentleness and the utmost care. I know they are not after my whole eye, just the bit of dust. I know they love me because they have assured me of that love. They have not written me off as worthless because they have exhorted me, commending me for what is right about our ministry. I realize they know the problem is with my eye and not with my heart, and that means so much to me. You see, it's one thing to point out a brother's error. It's another thing to condemn his heart.

I remember receiving a letter from a woman who had regularly taken part in our Precept Bible Studies over the years. She had listened to me teach again and again, so she certainly should have known my heart. Yet her letter was very censorious. She took offense because I had said I'd been prostrate on my face before the Lord in prayer, beseeching Him to give me His message, to speak through me. She thought it was prideful for me to talk about seeking the Lord in prayer this way, about weeping before Him, about longing for His message.

She had missed my heart! She didn't understand the total impotence, the utter poverty of spirit I feel as one who is accountable for the way I handle God's Word. Since then, she has criticized me on other matters. And do you know what? She has a *reputation* for criticizing teachers. It's like a log in her eye. Because of it, she cannot see how to take the speck out of someone else's eye.

We so often project our own problem upon others, don't we? What's worse, we frequently don't even know we *have* a problem!

How well this is illustrated in the Book of Romans. In Romans 1, Paul gives a clear picture of the degradation to which unsaved Gentiles can descend. As he writes his letter to those in Rome, however, the seasoned apostle knows his audience comprises not only Gentiles, but also Jews. At that point, in his mind's eye, Paul can see the Jews nodding their heads with approval.

"That's right, Paul. Go after them! Those Gentiles are really depraved. Such immorality! Such greed! Such murder! Such malice! They're *goyim!* Heathen of the worst sort. Gentile dogs, scavengers of garbage."

Paul knows the mind of self-righteous Jews. After all, he had been a self-righteous Jew himself! So in Romans 2, he turns to the Jews and exposes *their* guiltiness.

Read the following passage, marking every occurrence of the words *judge* and *judgment*.

➤ ROMANS 2:1-6, 17-24

Therefore you are without excuse, every man *of you* who passes judgment, for in that you judge another, you condemn yourself; for you who judge practice the same things. And we know that the judgment of God rightly falls upon those who practice such things. And do you suppose this, O man, when you pass judgment upon those who practice such things and do the same *yourself*, that you will escape the judgment of God? Or do you think lightly of the riches of His kindness and forbearance and patience, not knowing that the kindness of God leads you to repentance? But because of your stubbornness and unrepentant heart you are storing up wrath for yourself in the day of wrath and revelation of the righteous judgment of God, who WILL RENDER TO EVERY MAN ACCORDING TO HIS DEEDS.;

But if you bear the name "Jew," and rely upon the Law, and boast in God, and know *His* will, and approve the things that are essential, being instructed out of the Law, and are confident that you yourself are a guide to the blind, a light to those who are in darkness, a corrector of the foolish, a teacher of the immature, having in the Law the embodiment of knowledge and of the truth, you, therefore, who teach another, do you not teach yourself? You who preach that one should not steal, do you steal? You who say that one should not commit adultery, do you commit adultery? You who abhor idols, do you rob temples? You who boast in the Law, through your breaking the Law, do you dishonor

God? For "THE NAME OF GOD IS BLASPHEMED AMONG THE GEN-
TILES BECAUSE OF YOU," just as it is written.

Now list below any parallels you see between this passage in Romans
and what Jesus is saying in Matthew 7:1–5.

If, then, we are not to judge, how are we to deal with a brother in sin
and not violate Matthew 7:1? The Word of God clearly teaches that if we see
our brother caught in a trespass or straying from the truth, it is our responsibility in love to turn that brother back to a walk of righteousness.
Obviously to do so we have to discern that our brother is straying from the
truth.

1. In James 5:19–20, God's Word says:

> My brethren, if any among you strays from the truth, and one turns
> him back, let him know that he who turns a sinner from the error of
> his way will save his soul from death, and will cover a multitude of
> sins.

a. What are God's specific instructions in these verses?

b. How will it benefit the one who has strayed?

2. In Galatians 6:1, Paul writes:

> Brethren, even if a man is caught in any trespass, you who are spiritual, restore such a one in a spirit of gentleness; *each one* looking to yourself, lest you too be tempted.

a. What does this verse instruct us to do?

b. What does the verse say about the spiritual state of the restorer?

c. How is he to restore the one who has strayed?

Do James 5:19-20 and Galatians 6:1 directly violate God's command to us in Matthew 7? Of course not! Because Scripture cannot contradict Scripture. What then is the answer? Are we to judge or not to judge?

The answer is *in yourself*, the one who is judging. What is your walk with Jesus Christ like? Are you like those in Romans 2 who judged others, yet practiced the very same thing? Are you like those in Matthew 7, who went after little bits of dust in their brothers' eyes while they were afflicted with two-by-fours in their own? Have you met the qualifications of Galatians 6:1? "Brethren, even if a man is caught in any trespass, you who are spiritual, restore such a one in a spirit of gentleness; *each one* looking to yourself, lest you too be tempted."

I do not believe God is forbidding the discernment and removal of specks and motes. Specks should and can be removed from others' eyes as long as the eye surgery is done in a spirit of gentleness by one who is spiritual — one who is not there to condemn but to *restore.*

There's a big difference!

If we will do what Paul says in Galatians 6:1 and look to ourselves lest we also be tempted, this will keep us from an attitude of condemnation. We must always realize that we could have fallen, too! The flesh is the flesh, and any Christian who does not walk in the Spirit will fulfill the lust of the flesh (Galatians 5:16). It is essential, therefore, that whenever we seek to restore a fellow believer we realize that we could also have been tempted to sin. We cannot have a holier-than-thou attitude. To do so would violate Matthew 7:1 and Galatians 6:1.

Many a time I have sat with dear brothers and sisters who have become ensnared by the devil because they gave in to the lust of their flesh. My heart was grieved over their sin. I winced to think of the blasphemy it would bring to the name of God. They were wrong. They knew it. And yet, though sometimes I sat in the role of disciplinarian, I wept for them and with them and expressed my understanding. After all, I live in a body of flesh, too!

As I write this, I cannot help but think of our great High Priest, tempted in all points as we are, yet without sin, the One who did not come to judge but to save (Hebrews 4:15; John 3:17).

The next time, Beloved, that we see a speck in our brothers' eyes, let's remember to examine our own hearts first. Is our judgment for the purpose of condemnation or restoration? As we seek to restore, will we go in meekness, gentleness? If we'll answer these questions honestly, we'll know where we stand in our relationship to Matthew 7:1–5.

DAY THREE

Dear Betrayer...

My, that is a strong salutation, isn't it? As I've wrestled with this letter for weeks, however, I cannot address you in any other way. As a graduate of Precept Training, as a teacher of Precept, and as a recruiter for Precept classes and seminars, I can tell you that I've been committed to Precept Ministries and IBS, but am withdrawing this support now!

As you might imagine, I felt sick when I opened this letter. Martha, my wonderful and loving secretary, called me and warned me it was coming. Martha doesn't have any stars in her eyes when it comes to working with Kay Arthur. She's been around this ministry and me from our beginning "barn loft" days. She's younger than I am, but we've grown up together as the ministry has expanded from local Bible studies to a worldwide ministry. Martha knows me. Yet Martha loves me and doesn't appreciate anyone picking on me unjustly.

"Kay," she said on the phone, "I hate to pass this letter along to you."

And frankly I hated to get it. But that's part of ministry and part of leadership. I needed to see the letter. It was from a man who had been associated with our ministry for a number of years — a man who had sat under our ministry, participated in our Bible studies, and even taught a few of them. Yet he chose to begin his letter with the piercing word "Betrayer." And he ended his letter by saying he would no longer be part of our ministry but would instead become our adversary.

He had received a report from others about a teaching time I had with some young people he had ministered to, and he didn't like what he heard I'd done. As I looked back on the situation, I had to agree with some of the things he was saying. I could have handled the situation better. Some mistakes were made. What concerned me most, however, was this man's extremely harsh, blanket condemnation of me — without even giving me an opportunity to explain the situation. Why was he so ready to swing that gavel of judgment and completely sever our relationship?

I had to respond to this man's letter. But how? I prayed and then wrote a sweet letter, thanking him for writing and agreeing, to a degree. Then I wrote:

> However right or wrong I was, it's so hard to understand how you would allow one report from teenagers to destroy our association because of one mistake on my part. As a brother in Christ, and having the knowledge of what we teach and what we stand for, don't you believe God would have you come directly to me and say, "This is what

I have heard. Could you help verify it or explain it?" or "Kay, this is not typical of you. What happened?" It grieves my heart to think you would immediately dismiss me and the ministry without any grace to cover "my sin" or "my transgression." All of those years we have ministered together went down the drain in one single act, an act that isn't true to our reputation or standard, which I feel you should know after years of association. This is what hurts the most.

Do you truly believe this is the way the Lord would deal with this kind of situation? I may be wrong, but I don't think Jesus would deal with me this way. Nor do I think Paul would, on the basis of 2 Timothy 2:24–26. One of my concerns is, if you will deal with me this way, how will you deal with others on the mission field who fail or make mistakes? Are mistakes fatal so that we are written off, spoken against, and called "Betrayer"?

After several more paragraphs I closed by saying:

I hope you will give me the opportunity to talk with you. It grieves my heart to be judged in this manner without an opportunity to share with you what we were trying to accomplish.

Seven weeks later, Martha called the house. "Kay…Kay, I hate to interrupt you, but you are going to be so excited. We got the most wonderful letter, Kay. You're going to be so happy. It's from the young man who wrote you that terrible letter."

"Read it, Martha! Read it!"

Martha read…and I cried.

Dear Kay,

Thank you for your letter of September 25. It was kind of you to respond personally to my concerns, especially in light of the inappropriate way in which I brought them to you. I want to thank you for your loving reproof of my manner of attacking you regarding the situation with my former youth group. I've repented before the Lord and would ask your forgiveness for this sin against you. I've much to learn as to how to handle situations like these, and your letter has helped me to grow in this area. Thank you for allowing the Lord to use you, in spite of the hurt which I caused you, to make me more like Him.

And the letter went on— closing this way:

May the Lord continue to use you and the staff of Precept Ministries to advance His Kingdom as you establish His people in His Word. I would appreciate continuing our association in the future if you feel that it is appropriate. Thank you for your prayers.

Sincerely, in Christ.

As soon as I hung up, I had my stationery out, dashing off a note to this man, telling him how very proud I was of him and how I could "hug the puddin' out of him." (I can talk that way. I'm sixty-two!)

Many times our judging is wrong because either we don't judge in love or we judge according to our own standard of behavior. This is what we will look at today. Will you come to God with a teachable spirit, Beloved, even as this precious young man did?

The Jews were angry with Jesus. He was not honoring the Sabbath! Obviously He could not be from God. Jesus sensed their anger so He confronted them:

> "If a man receives circumcision on *the* Sabbath that the Law of Moses may not be broken, are you angry with Me because I made an entire man well on *the* Sabbath? Do not judge according to appearance, but judge with righteous judgment." (John 7:23–24)

Isn't that the way it is today, Beloved? We look at people and feel upset that their behavior does not conform to *our* standards of spirituality. Notice I said "our standards," not God's, for we, like the Pharisees, have added our own traditions to the Word of God.

We may say, no, God didn't speak clearly in Scripture on this particular "issue," but *surely* anyone who *truly* loves God wouldn't be doing what they are doing!

Or if we don't judge their behavior, we judge their personality. We decide that they aren't Christlike because they don't seem sober enough; they kid too much. And nobody could be humble and have such authority, such confidence!

Or maybe it's their style of dress; it's too contemporary. Or maybe it's their...whatever! You name it — it's something you disapprove of, although there is no clear or direct violation of the Word — even in principle. And therefore (you think), surely it could not be spiritual! And so you judge.

What are we doing, Beloved? *We're doing the same thing the Pharisees did in Jesus' day.* We are judging on the basis of appearance. They forgot what God said to Samuel: "God *sees* not as man sees, for man looks at the outward appearance, but the LORD looks at the heart" (1 Samuel 16:7). It is easy for man to judge according to appearance; it's difficult for him to judge with righteous judgment!

The Jews were judging Jesus on the basis of their interpretation of the Law. In the process, they actually became the offenders of the Law. James 4:11–12 says:

> Do not speak against one another, brethren. He who speaks against a brother, or judges his brother, speaks against the law, and judges the law; but if you judge the law, you are not a doer of the law, but a judge *of it.* There is *only* one Lawgiver and Judge, the One who is able to save and to destroy; but who are you who judge your neighbor?

The minute you and I sit in condemnation against another, we are speaking against the Law, and we are judging the Law. Why? Because the Law finds its fulfillment in love, not judgment.

> Owe nothing to anyone except to love one another; for he who loves his neighbor has fulfilled *the* law.... and if there is any other commandment, it is summed up in this saying, "YOU SHALL LOVE YOUR NEIGHBOR AS YOURSELF." Love does no wrong to a neighbor, love therefore is the fulfillment of *the* law. (Romans 13:8–10)

How can you tell if you are judging with righteous judgment rather than according to appearance? How can you tell whether or not you are breaking Jesus' command in Matthew 7:1?

You will know, Beloved, by your attitude.

What is your motivation? Is love of God missing? Is love of your neighbor missing? Are you concerned about that speck in your brother's eye in a condemning way? If any of these things is true, you can know that you are judging the Law and breaking Jesus' commandment not to judge.

So many Christians violate the principle of love — and it tears the heart out of their Christian testimony. Did not Jesus say, "By this all men will know that you are My disciples, if you have love for one another" (John 13:35)?

Judging without love is often a symptom of patching together our own code or standard for righteousness. We develop a set of dos and don'ts that determine a man's or woman's spiritual status — and then we seek to impose these upon others. I think this is what Jesus is warning us against in the Sermon on the Mount. He knows the weakness of our flesh. He knows that as He calls us to this high standard of living it is apt to make us judgmental. How right He is!

In Romans 14, Paul has to address the same problem.

Who are you to judge the servant of another? To his own master he stands or falls; and stand he will, for the Lord is able to make him stand. (Romans 14:4)

When Jews and Gentiles were merged into one body, the Jews brought with them their legalism. The Gentiles brought with them their freedom — they had never lived under the Law. This created a major problem. Each had a different standard of holiness, and this resulted in judging.

Romans 14:1–15:1 is printed out for you. As you read through this chapter, mark the following key words, each in their own way. First, mark every reference to the "weak in faith," including pronouns. These terms represent the Jewish believers. Then mark every reference to the others Paul is referring to — those who are being judged by the weak. Romans 15:1 refers to them as "the strong." The third thing you need to mark is the word *judge* or *judgment*.

➤ ROMANS 14:1–15:1

1 Now accept the one who is weak in faith, *but* not for *the purpose of* passing judgment on his opinions.

2 One man has faith that he may eat all things, but he who is weak eats vegetables *only*.

3 Let not him who eats regard with contempt him who does not eat, and let not him who does not eat judge him who eats, for God has accepted him.

4 Who are you to judge the servant of another? To his own master he stands or falls; and stand he will, for the Lord is able to make him stand.

5 One man regards one day above another, another regards every day *alike*. Let each man be fully convinced in his own mind.

6 He who observes the day, observes it for the Lord, and he who eats, does so for the Lord, for he gives thanks to God; and he who eats not, for the Lord he does not eat, and gives thanks to God.

7 For not one of us lives for himself, and not one dies for himself;

8 for if we live, we live for the Lord, or if we die, we die for the Lord; therefore whether we live or die, we are the Lord's.

9 For to this end Christ died and lived *again,* that He might be Lord both of the dead and of the living.

10 But you, why do you judge your brother? Or you again, why do you regard your brother with contempt? For we shall all stand before the judgment seat of God.

11 For it is written,

"AS I LIVE, SAYS THE LORD, EVERY KNEE SHALL BOW TO ME,

AND EVERY TONGUE SHALL GIVE PRAISE TO GOD."

12 So then each one of us shall give account of himself to God.

13 Therefore let us not judge one another anymore, but rather determine this — not to put an obstacle or a stumbling block in a brother's way.

14 I know and am convinced in the Lord Jesus that nothing is unclean in itself; but to him who thinks anything to be unclean, to him it is unclean.

15 For if because of food your brother is hurt, you are no longer walking according to love. Do not destroy with your food him for whom Christ died.

16 Therefore do not let what is for you a good thing be spoken of as evil;

17 for the kingdom of God is not eating and drinking, but righteousness and peace and joy in the Holy Spirit.

18 For he who in this *way* serves Christ is acceptable to God and approved by men.

19 So then let us pursue the things which make for peace and the building up of one another.

20 Do not tear down the work of God for the sake of food. All things indeed are clean, but they are evil for the man who eats and gives offense.

21 It is good not to eat meat or to drink wine, or *to do anything* by which your brother stumbles.

22 The faith which you have, have as your own conviction before God. Happy is he who does not condemn himself in what he approves.

23 But he who doubts is condemned if he eats, because *his eating* is not from faith; and whatever is not from faith is sin.

1 Now we who are strong ought to bear the weaknesses of those without strength and not *just* please ourselves.

1. What is the problem described in Romans 14:1–3?

2. What is the problem in verses 5–6?

3. According to verse 15, how are we to walk?

4. What are God's instructions regarding judging in this area of differences?

5. What are we to pursue, according to verse 19?

6. How are we to walk regarding our own convictions? Read verses 20–23.

Much of our problem in judging is in this area, isn't it? This gray area of dos, don'ts, and differences, all depending on our religious upbringing or lack of it. We need to remember that "the kingdom of God is not eating and drinking, but righteousness and peace and joy in the Holy Spirit" (Romans 14:17). If we walk according to love and pursue the things that make for peace and for the building up of one another, then we need not worry about breaking Jesus' commandment in Matthew 7:1.

> Therefore do not go on passing judgment before the time, *but wait* until the Lord comes who will both bring to light the things hidden in the darkness and disclose the motives of *men's* hearts; and then each man's praise will come to him from God. (1 Corinthians 4:5)

O Beloved, go before the throne of grace and ask God to examine your heart.

Are you sitting as a judge, speaking against the Law and therefore judging the Law because you are not walking in love toward your brother?

Are you seeking to judge the motives of people's hearts where you can only see their outward appearance?

Have you, like the Pharisees, added your tradition to God's Word and then sought to judge another individual's walk with God according to your interpretation of the Law?

Have you done eye surgery with great humility and gentleness...or did you have a holier-than-thou attitude? Did you realize that you yourself could be tempted also?

Do you need to admit that you are wrong? Do you need to go to anyone and ask his or her forgiveness? Ask God to show you your heart, Beloved, and then whatever the Spirit of God says to do, do it. You won't be sorry.

DAY FOUR

When Jesus said, "Do not judge lest you be judged," was He calling us to a blithe blindness to the unrighteous behavior of others?

Was He calling us to close our eyes to sin, to tolerate false doctrines and indiscriminately accept those who teach them?

Was He telling us to take the beautiful gems of the gospel and throw them before swine that they might trample them in the mud?

Was He calling us to share the precious truths of God's Word with those whom we know will only mock and ridicule them, making fun of our beliefs?

We need answers to these questions. And those answers can only come as we look at the whole counsel of the Word of God. So study well, Beloved. I know this is a heavy week, but it will be so profitable to the kingdom of God. Do your assignments diligently. And as you do them, don't forget to go to your Teacher, the Holy Spirit. Ask Him to lead you into all truth, and as you do, remember He will never contradict the Word of God.

Now then, let's compare scripture with scripture.

Matthew 7:6 tells us:

"Do not give what is holy to dogs, and do not throw your pearls before swine, lest they trample them under their feet, and turn and tear you to pieces."

1. What is Jesus warning us about in this verse? (There's no "secret answer" here. I just want you to state what you observe in the text.)

2. Now, listen to Philippians 3:2–3, 17–19.

Beware of the dogs, beware of the evil workers, beware of the false circumcision; for we are the *true* circumcision, who worship in the Spirit of God and glory in Christ Jesus and put no confidence in the flesh....

Brethren, join in following my example, and observe those who walk according to the pattern you have in us. For many walk, of whom I often told you, and now tell you even weeping, that they are enemies of the cross of Christ, whose end is destruction, whose god is their appetite, and whose glory is their shame, who set their minds on earthly things.

    a. Do these verses call for any judgment or discernment on your part? How?

    b. How do these verses in Philippians compare with Matthew 7:6?

3. Now let's compare what you've learned from Matthew 7:6 and the verses in Philippians 3 with 2 Peter 2:1–2.

But false prophets also arose among the people, just as there will also be false teachers among you, who will secretly introduce destructive heresies, even denying the Master who bought them, bringing swift destruction upon themselves. And many will follow their sensuality, and because of them the way of the truth will be maligned.

Write out your observations below.

Swine have no appreciation for pearls, whatsoever. And dogs? The dogs referred to in the Bible are not the lovable, well-trained, household pets you and I think of. The dogs of Jesus' day were savage, wild curs that roamed the streets and hills of Palestine, foraging for food and intimidating anyone who would keep them from filling their bellies with garbage. That which was holy meant nothing to them; their god was their appetite.

Pigs who lived in the mire could not appreciate beautiful pearls, and dogs who ate their own vomit certainly had no regard for what was holy. Jesus' hearers understood very well what He was saying when He talked about dogs and pigs!

The theme of 2 Peter 2 is false teachers. Although we will study this chapter in greater detail next week, I want you to see how God compares these false teachers to dogs and sows. Listen to verse 22 where *them* refers to the false teachers:

It has happened to them, according to the true proverb, "A DOG RETURNS TO ITS OWN VOMIT" and "A sow, after washing, *returns* to wallowing in the mire."

From 2 Peter 2 and Matthew 7:15–20 where Jesus warns his listeners to beware of false prophets, it should be obvious that we have to judge who are the false prophets and false teachers! If we are warned not to put pearls before swine nor holy things before dogs, then it's obvious we will have to exercise some discernment to identify these pigs and dogs. Do we have the right, then, to evaluate carefully a person's message? Do we have the right to scrutinize someone's teaching? Is doctrine that important?

Listen to 1 John 4:1–6.

Beloved, do not believe every spirit, but test the spirits to see whether they are from God; because many false prophets have gone out into the world. By this you know the Spirit of God: every spirit that confesses that Jesus Christ has come in the flesh is from God; and every spirit that does not confess Jesus is not from God; and this is the *spirit* of the antichrist, of which you have heard that it is coming, and now it is already in the world. You are from God, little children, and have overcome them; because greater is He who is in you than he who is in the world. They are from the world; therefore they speak *as* from the world, and the world listens to them. We are from God; he who knows

God listens to us; he who is not from God does not listen to us. By this we know the spirit of truth and the spirit of error.

1. How does this passage compare with Matthew 7:15–20 and 1 Peter 2:21–22?

2. What is God's instruction to us in this passage?

3. According to 1 John 4:1–6, are we responsible to discern between the Spirit of truth and the spirit of error?

I once heard a popular Christian broadcaster say on the air, "Don't give me any of that doctrinal doo-doo." Is doctrine important? It is *essential*, Beloved. According to 2 Timothy 3:16, "All Scripture is inspired by God and profitable for teaching...." The problem is that many won't take the time or discipline necessary to learn what they believe. Their doctrine comes from others, rather than from the Word of God. For this reason, it is easier for them to become ensnared by false teaching.

Just turn on a lot of Christian television, and it will become immediately obvious to you as you see what they "amen," get excited about, and support financially. How it breaks my heart! How I grieve when I see them sending in hundreds of thousands of dollars to support what they know so little about. They have so little discernment because they simply don't know God's Word for themselves. Instead, they feed on excitement, sweet and touching stories, dreams, visions, and dramatic accounts of miracles — all "chaff" in comparison to the pure "wheat" of God's Word.

Look up the following scriptures in your own Bible. Note what each says about wrong doctrine (teaching) and your responsibility, if any. Record your answers in the space provided. When you look up these verses in your Bible, be sure to mark them so you can easily spot them when you need them.

1. Ephesians 4:14

2. 1 Timothy 1:3–4

3. 1 Timothy 4:1–3, 6

4. 2 Timothy 4:2–4

Those who belong to the kingdom of heaven are not to sit as censorious judges, but they are to be discriminating about whom they follow. They are also to be discriminating about sharing God's precious truths. To fail to discriminate would mean that truth would be trampled upon.

Are we to judge? Yes, we are to judge with just judgment. God's kind of judgment. But you can only discern what is wrong by knowing truth. How do you measure up? Let me urge you, Beloved, to continue to study His Word diligently. It is imperative, Beloved, that you know the whole counsel of God in these last days.

<hr/>

D A Y   F I V E

To judge or not to judge, that is the question! Or perhaps I should say, *that is the confusion.* But that fog of confusion should be lifting after this week's study. God willing, you will be seeing some blue sky and sunshine!

Here is one of the questions remaining with us: What else, if anything, are you and I to judge?

Let's search the Scriptures so you can see for yourself exactly what God wants you to judge. Read the verses that follow. As you read, record, underline, or note in some way beneficial to you, what you are to judge or discern and how you are to do it. (If the text tells you!)

➤ 2 THESSALONIANS 3:6, 11, 14–15

Now we command you, brethren, in the name of our Lord Jesus Christ, that you keep aloof from every brother who leads an unruly life and not according to the tradition which you received from us.... For we hear that some among you are leading an undisciplined life, doing no work at all, but acting like busybodies.... And if anyone does not obey our instruction in this letter, take special note of that man and do not associate with him, so that he may be put to shame. And *yet* do not regard him as an enemy, but admonish him as a brother.

➤ 1 CORINTHIANS 5:1-3, 9-13

It is actually reported that there is immorality among you, and immorality of such a kind as does not exist even among the Gentiles, that someone has his father's wife. And you have become arrogant, and have not mourned instead, in order that the one who had done this deed might be removed from your midst. For I, on my part, though absent in body but present in spirit, have already judged him who has so committed this, as though I were present.…

I wrote you in my letter not to associate with immoral people; I *did* not at all *mean* with the immoral people of this world, or with the covetous and swindlers, or with idolaters; for then you would have to go out of the world. But actually, I wrote to you not to associate with any so-called brother if he should be an immoral person, or covetous, or an idolater, or a reviler, or a drunkard, or a swindler — not even to eat with such a one. For what have I to do with judging outsiders? Do you not judge those who are within *the church?* But those who are outside, God judges. REMOVE THE WICKED MAN FROM AMONG YOURSELVES.

➤ MATTHEW 18:15-20

"And if your brother sins, go and reprove him in private; if he listens to you, you have won your brother. But if he does not listen *to you,* take one or two more with you, so that BY THE MOUTH OF TWO OR THREE WITNESSES EVERY FACT MAY BE CONFIRMED. And if he refuses to listen to them, tell it to the church; and if he refuses to listen even to the church, let him be to you as a Gentile and a tax-gatherer. Truly I say to you, whatever you shall bind on earth shall be bound in heaven; and whatever you loose on earth shall be loosed in heaven. Again I say to you, that if two of you agree on earth about anything that they may ask, it shall be done for them by My Father who is in heaven. For where two or three have gathered together in My name, there I am in their midst."

➤ HEBREWS 5:14

But solid food is for the mature, who because of practice have their senses trained to discern good and evil.

➤ 1 CORINTHIANS 11:27–32

Therefore whoever eats the bread or drinks the cup of the Lord in an unworthy manner, shall be guilty of the body and the blood of the Lord. But let a man examine himself, and so let him eat of the bread and drink of the cup. For he who eats and drinks, eats and drinks judgment to himself, if he does not judge the body rightly. For this reason many among you are weak and sick, and a number sleep. But if we judged ourselves rightly, we should not be judged. But when we are judged, we are disciplined by the Lord in order that we may not be condemned along with the world.

A careful study of these scriptures — including Matthew 7:1–5 — shows that judging is not forbidden. Irresponsible behavior, wrong doctrine, and sin must all be discerned, clearly identified, and dealt with. They are not to be swallowed, covered over, winked at, or overlooked. Righteousness is to be upheld, the gospel is to be earnestly contended for. Judging, therefore, is not wrong if it is done properly. It is fine to correct a brother as long as you do it in a spirit of gentleness, as long as you are spiritual, realizing that you are not above temptation yourself. It is all right to judge as long as the motivation of that judgment is love of God and love of your neighbor. The goal of judgment, remember, is not to condemn but to restore.

It is all right to judge as long as we judge with a righteous judgment, a judgment that is in accordance with God's Word. We may judge dogs and swine, false prophets, sin, wrong behavior, and wrong doctrine. But we cannot judge the motives of a man's or woman's heart.

But above all, Beloved, we must continuously judge ourselves! As Paul notes, "If we judged ourselves rightly, we should not be judged" (1 Corinthians 11:31). Let's make sure the beam is out of our own eyes. This is the message of Matthew 7:1–5.

O Father...

Who can understand *his* errors? Cleanse thou me from secret *faults*. Keep back thy servant also from presumptuous *sins*; let them not have dominion over me: then shall I be upright, and I shall be innocent from the great transgression. Let the words of my mouth, and the meditation of my heart, be acceptable in thy sight, O LORD, my strength, and my redeemer. (Psalm 19:12–14, KJV)

Search me, O God, and know my heart: try me, and know my thoughts: and see if *there be any* wicked way in me, and lead me in the way everlasting. (Psalm 139:23–24, KJV)

DO YOU POSSESS THE KINGDOM OF HEAVEN?

DAY ONE

Have you ever despaired of being "perfect, even as your Father in heaven is perfect"?

Have you ever cried out with Paul, "Who is adequate for these things?"

Have you ever looked up into the stars at night and said with David, "It is too high. I cannot attain to it"?

Have you ever looked into your own heart and sighed, "Oh, God, when will I ever learn?"

Have you groaned, longing to be clothed with your new body from heaven, finally free of the flesh that keeps causing you to stumble?

Have you ever feared that someday you might stumble and never get up?

I understand, my friend.

I understand because I too live in a body of flesh. I know that although my spirit may be willing, my flesh is often all too weak.

Even more important, *Jesus* understands! He understands because He too lived in a body of flesh. As a man, He experienced the reality that the spirit is willing but the flesh is weak. He walked where you walk. He sat where you sit. "You have a High Priest who can be touched with the feeling of your infirmities."

Jesus realizes that in the Sermon on the Mount He has set a righteousness before you which is impossible apart from Him. Who can reach this
high level of righteousness? Who can walk where Jesus has walked? Only
the poor in spirit, those who have acknowledged their utter spiritual
poverty. Only those who have attained the kingdom of heaven and have
been filled by God's own Spirit have a righteousness that exceeds that of the
scribes and Pharisees.

Matthew 7:7–12 is printed out so you can keep the text immediately
before you. As you read through this passage, underline each of our Lord's
instructions in this portion of the Sermon. Keep your eyes open for the keys
to a life of righteousness that pleases God.

➤ MATTHEW 7:7–12

7 "Ask, and it shall be given to you; seek, and you shall find; knock, and
it shall be opened to you.

8 "For everyone who asks receives, and he who seeks finds, and to him
who knocks it shall be opened.

9 "Or what man is there among you, when his son shall ask him for a
loaf, will he give him a stone?

10 "Or if he shall ask for a fish, he will not give him a snake, will he?

11 "If you then, being evil, know how to give good gifts to your children, how much more shall your Father who is in heaven give what is
good to those who ask Him!

12 "Therefore, however you want people to treat you, so treat them, for
this is the Law and the Prophets."

What keys to a life of righteousness did you notice as you read this passage?

In verses 7–11 we see keys in our relationship toward God in the three words *asking, seeking,* and *knocking.* Each of these words is in the present tense in Greek, indicating a continuous or habitual action. In verse 12 we see the key in our relationships toward fellow human beings in the instruction to treat others as we want them to treat us.

The Christian life is to be lived in total dependence upon God. The greater the dependence, the greater the righteousness. Let me repeat that for emphasis: *The greater the dependence, the greater the righteousness.* Keep on asking, Jesus tells us. Keep on seeking. Keep on knocking. This is a life of persistent dependence.

Let's slow down and think this through for a few moments. If you and I want what is "good," where will it be found? God is the only One who is good. Therefore, we come to our Father. Because He *is* our Father and because He *is* good, He wants us to have what is good. For this reason, we need to keep on asking and it will be given to us, to keep on seeking and we will find, to keep on knocking and it will be opened to us. He is our heavenly Father who delights to give what is good to those who ask Him.

Luke 11 sets before us the same truth of Matthew 7:7–12. It is preceded, however, by a very pertinent illustration which I want us to look at. Read Luke 11:5–13, printed out for you. As you read, mark every use of the word *friend.*

➤ LUKE 11:5-13

And He said to them, "Suppose one of you shall have a friend, and shall go to him at midnight, and say to him, 'Friend, lend me three loaves; for a friend of mine has come to me from a journey, and I have nothing to set before him'; and from inside he shall answer and say, 'Do not bother me; the door has already been shut and my children and I are in bed; I cannot get up and give you *anything.*' I tell you, even though he will not get up and give him *anything* because he is his friend, yet because of his persistence he will get up and give him as much as he needs. And I say to you, ask, and it shall be given to you; seek, and you shall find; knock, and it shall be opened to you. For everyone who asks, receives; and he who seeks, finds; and to him who knocks, it shall be opened. Now suppose one of you fathers is asked by his son for a fish; he will not give him a snake instead of a fish, will he? Or *if* he is asked for an egg, he will not give him a scorpion, will he? If you then, being evil, know how to give good gifts to your children, how much more shall *your* heavenly Father give the Holy Spirit to those who ask Him?"

Now then, let's answer some questions from the text.

1. Did the man's friendship have anything to do with giving his friend three loaves of bread?

2. How or why did the man get his bread?

3. When Jesus told the story, do you think He was trying to tell us that even though He's our friend, He is reluctant to give us what we need? Explain your answer.

4. What is the point Jesus wants to make in this story? What does He want His children to see?

Jesus wants us to see the importance and reward of persistence. He reassures us that our persistence will pay off because of the character of the One to whom we are coming. He is more than an earthly parent. If earthly parents — those with natural affections — will not do their children harm, will not our heavenly Father who is perfect give even more love, care, and provision? Because He is the Father of fathers — the very epitome of fatherhood — it is His highest pleasure to give us what is good. Earthly fathers, for the most part, seek to give their children good things. How much more will our heavenly Father give us what is good?

You may have noticed that the passage in Luke 11 talks about the heavenly Father giving the Holy Spirit to those who ask Him. I don't want to take off on a tangent, and yet I want to make sure you don't go off on one of your own either! So let me simply state some facts you need to consider.

At this point in the economy of God, as Jesus spoke to his disciples, the Holy Spirit had not yet come to indwell believers because Jesus had not yet gone to the Father (John 14:16–18, 26; 16:7, 13). For this reason, they were to ask for the Holy Spirit. Jesus was *not* telling you and me, who already have the Holy Spirit through salvation, that we need to ask for the Spirit again. At that point in time, the disciples were on one side — the B.C. side — of the death, burial, resurrection, and ascension of Jesus Christ. As disciples today, we are on the other side, the A.D. side.

For us, Pentecost has come and gone. We who have entered the New Covenant receive the Holy Spirit the moment we receive Jesus Christ as our Lord and Savior. Once you are saved, then, you don't need to keep asking for the Holy Spirit. He is already within you (Romans 8:1–17). The need of your life and mine is to *keep walking in persistent dependence upon God*, allowing ourselves to be filled and controlled by His Spirit (see Ephesians 5:18).

Now then, Beloved, what do you personally need in order to live this life of righteousness God has called you to? Whatever it is, *keep on asking Him for it*. Your Father promises that it will be given to you. Whatever you are seeking as a child of God that you need in order to please your Father and do His work, keep on seeking it. Don't stop! He promises you will find it.

What is closed to you that needs to be opened? Keep on knocking for it to be opened. Keep on knocking, and knocking, and knocking at that closed door. It will open. It has to, because God promised — and He is God. What you need is yours because it is His, and your heavenly Father delights to give you good gifts.

Have you ever read the book *Of Whom the World Was Not Worthy* by Marie Chapian? I cannot recommend it highly enough. This biography will stir your soul and drive you to your knees. It beautifully illustrates the principle of persistent dependence upon our heavenly Father.

The author tells the story of Jakob and Jozeca, simple Yugoslavian peasants who loved the Lord Jesus and whose lives were filled by the Spirit of God. Jakob and Jozeca prayed and prayed until God gave them a son. Josip, the answer to their persistent praying, was to be a man of God. Jozeca was convinced of this. Therefore, when her son at the age of eleven was run over by a truck and pronounced dead, Jozeca threw her body on top of Josip's and began breathing into his mouth, crying, "He is not dead! God did not bring us this far to take his life away! I will not accept it! Never!"

For one hour she breathed into a pulseless body until finally the color came back to his skin. As Josip healed from his injuries, however, it became obvious that he was no longer normal. Although doctors could find no brain damage, the boy suffered over 150 terrible seizures during the next five years. He was hospitalized thirty-three times in three different hospitals. Each time Jozeca refused to believe the situation was hopeless.

"God gave us this son to train for His glory. Then He raised him up when he had been proclaimed dead. I cannot believe He brought him into this world to be sick in the mind!"

The seizures came most often during the night, so night after night she remained on her knees by his bed, praying until his breathing became regular again. In a desperate attempt to do all she could for her son, she even slept with him in bed at night and lined up her feet with his so the soles of their feet were touching. That way she could feel if his nerves twitched, and she would leap up and shout, "Josip! Wake up! Come, son, wake up! Praise the Lord, Josip! Wake up! Come, son, wake up! Praise the Lord, Josip! Wake up!" And the attack would be aborted.

When he was hospitalized, she was not allowed to visit him every day. So she stood beneath his window and whistled "God Is Love." He could hear her and know she was there, near him, praying for him. And Jakob, who worked in the mine from sunup to sundown, often remained on his knees all night in prayer. He would say to his wife:

"Jozeca, the Bible says, 'Ask and ye shall receive,' and we must believe that."

"But, Jakob, I have asked and asked and asked."

"Then ask again."

"I shall never stop asking, Jakob. Never. I believe God gave us this son to bring glory to His name. I believe He gave us this son to raise to be a minister of the Lord. I believe He will one day serve the Lord. I will never stop praying for this son of ours. Not until either he or I am no longer on this earth."[1]

Seven years would pass before that prayer was answered, but answered it was. God sent a believer from Russia to release Josip's body from the grip of the enemy. They had asked, they had sought, they had knocked, and finally they received. The door finally opened. It was not the last battle that Jakob and Jozeca would fight in prayer for Josip. He would be prayed through rebellion, through impending death, and eventually into a Baptist seminary and into the ministry.

O Beloved, what is yours because you are His? Pursue it persistently. Ask, seek, knock. Jesus is the One who tells you to do this. It is both a command and a loving invitation.

D A Y   T W O

Yesterday we looked at the vertical aspect of the life of righteousness. Our Lord invites us to keep on asking, seeking, and knocking.

Today we want to look at the horizontal aspect of that righteousness. A righteous walk with God will always manifest itself in our relationship with our fellow man. The two are inseparable, for our righteousness is demonstrated in our treatment of one another.

In Matthew 5:17, Jesus assured us that He did not come to abolish the Law or the Prophets but to fulfill them. Now He calls us to walk as He walked. As He fulfilled the Law, so are we to fulfill it. And how do we do this? The answer is in Matthew 7:12: "However you want people to treat you, so treat them, for this is the Law and the Prophets."

This is "The Golden Rule" we have heard so much about — the great rule of life so many say they try to live by. "Do unto others as you would have them do unto you."

Why do many try to live by this rule and yet fail miserably?

First of all, they fail to understand that in and of ourselves we cannot continuously live on this high and lofty plane. At the root of all sin is self-centeredness — and man apart from the Spirit of God cannot please God. True, some people are less self-centered than others. A great and admirable nobility can be achieved even among sinners. Many wonderful things have been accomplished by people who did not profess to know Jesus Christ. Numerous humanitarian efforts have been launched by people whose hearts were filled with compassion — even though they were not filled with the presence of the Holy Spirit.

Yet, with all their good deeds, these compassionate people could never fulfill the Law and the Prophets. Why? Because Scripture begins with honoring God as God, then treating others as God would have us treat them.

When you consider the Ten Commandments in Exodus 20, you may notice that the commandments first describe the relationship between God and man. The commandments begin with loving God, having no idols before Him, not taking His name in vain, and keeping the Sabbath day holy. Then, after those things have been established, the commandments go on to speak of the relationships between people. We are told to honor father and mother and not to murder, commit adultery, steal, bear false witness, or covet our neighbor's possessions.

We can see the same pattern when we compare the Beatitudes with the

Ten Commandments. The Beatitudes begin with our relationship to God, regarding poverty of spirit, mourning, meekness, and hungering and thirsting after righteousness. Then they turn toward our relationship with our fellow human beings, speaking of mercy, purity of heart, peacemaking, and our attitude toward persecution.

What truth is hidden in this order, in this priority toward God? I believe it is the truth of *being* rather than just *doing*. Doing always finds limits when it functions out of its own strength or according to its own moral code. Doing is limited by what we are. As natural man, we can never fulfill the Law and the Prophets. We will never quite do for others all that we want done for ourselves. But if I can change *what I am*, if I can be different from ordinary man, if I honor God as God and am inhabited by God, then I can do for others as I would have them do for me. I can love them, because the God who is love is in me. And when I love them, I fulfill the Law. According to James 2:8, it is the royal law...the law of our King. And when I live by the royal law, I fulfill the Law and the Prophets.

Read Matthew 22:34–40, which is printed out below. Mark every reference to love and to the Law (or commandment) in a distinctive way.

> But when the Pharisees heard that He had put the Sadducees to silence, they gathered themselves together. And one of them, a lawyer, asked Him *a question*, testing Him, "Teacher, which is the great commandment in the Law?" And He said to him, "'YOU SHALL LOVE THE LORD YOUR GOD WITH ALL YOUR HEART, AND WITH ALL YOUR SOUL, AND WITH ALL YOUR MIND.' This is the great and foremost commandment. The second is like it, 'YOU SHALL LOVE YOUR NEIGHBOR AS YOURSELF.' On these two commandments depend the whole Law and the Prophets."

Now, listen again to Romans 13:1–8. As you read it, mark *law (commandment)* and *love* in the same way.

> Let every person be in subjection to the governing authorities. For there is no authority except from God, and those which exist are established by God. Therefore he who resists authority has opposed the ordinance of

God; and they who have opposed will receive condemnation upon themselves. For rulers are not a cause of fear for good behavior, but for evil. Do you want to have no fear of authority? Do what is good, and you will have praise from the same; for it is a minister of God to you for good. But if you do what is evil, be afraid; for it does not bear the sword for nothing; for it is a minister of God, an avenger who brings wrath upon the one who practices evil. Wherefore it is necessary to be in subjection, not only because of wrath, but also for conscience' sake. For because of this you also pay taxes, for *rulers* are servants of God, devoting themselves to this very thing. Render to all what is due them: tax to whom tax *is due*; custom to whom custom; fear to whom fear; honor to whom honor. Owe nothing to anyone except to love one another; for he who loves his neighbor has fulfilled *the* law.

Now list below what you learned from marking *law* and *love* in these two passages.

To be sure we bring this full circle, let me ask you another question. Don't we all need and want love — unconditional love, love that desires our highest good? Then treat other people in precisely the same way *you* would want to be treated! This is the Law and the Prophets. This is fulfilling the Law.

I remember a night years ago when a group gathered at our home for a covered dish supper. Afterward we all headed for the Tivoli Theater to see the old movie *Bringing Up Baby*.

The Tivoli, a grand old theater that hosts operas, musicals, and other events, occasionally used to show some of the old, wholesome movies. It was like the old days — with twenty-five-cent bags of popcorn and a concert on the Wurlitzer organ before the movie started. That evening was a welcome relief after our long hours of work and perpetually tight schedules.

Following the movie we were laughing at the 1938 antics of Cary Grant and Katherine Hepburn and just having a time of sweet fellowship in the lobby with other Christians who had also needed a wholesome night out. My husband, Jack, and Clyde Hawkins, the manager of the Tivoli, had a long talk, so we were the last ones to leave the theater. As we were walking out one door, a man entered the other. His head hung down, and he carried a battered paper sack in his right hand. His walk was slow, steady, and deliberate — yet he seemed devoid of life and purpose. He walked past us as if we didn't exist. I took my eyes off of him, but I didn't want to. I couldn't believe his face! It was covered with red, raw gashes and two horizontal cuts that ran from ear to nose, as if someone had smashed him up against a concrete wall.

He walked by without a word and sat down on a bench. Immediately Clyde went back and said something to him, which we couldn't hear. The man got up and walked out of the theater just as he had come in.

We stepped outside and watched him walk away. Even as I write this, I can see him walking down the street. We stood there and talked about how horrible he looked, how sad he was. We were curious. We hurt. As we walked to the car, I said, "Oh the awful wages of sin."

But I never did for that man what I would have wanted done for me.

Today as I think about him again, even after all these years, the statement "no man cared for my soul" runs through my mind.

What should I have done? I really don't know. I only know this: I should have done *something*. In some way I should have reached out to that man.

Do you know why I didn't? Because I didn't take the time or opportunity to talk to my Father about it. I never asked my Father what I should do. To be honest, I was so taken aback, so shocked, I never even thought about it. And I am ashamed.

As I reflect on that situation now, I can guess that I was probably frozen in a state of inertia because my service to the Lord seem filled to capacity and overflowing already! The thought of lifting a finger and doing "one more thing" probably stymied me.

But do you know what, Beloved? That is no excuse at all. In every situation of life I need to learn and learn and learn *persistent dependence* upon my God, continually asking, continually seeking, continually knocking. This is when I must remember that if I am to walk as Jesus walked, fulfilling the Law and the Prophets, I must continually keep the highest good of others before me, doing unto them as I would have them do unto me.

Can you imagine what a difference it would make in our world if every child of God lived this way? It will never happen until you and I determine we will live this way.

D A Y   T H R E E

As we come to Matthew 7:13–14, it seems to me that we have come full circle. Jesus says,

> "Enter by the narrow gate; for the gate is wide, and the way is broad that leads to destruction, and many are those who enter by it. For the gate is small, and the way is narrow that leads to life, and few are those who find it."

How small is that gate? It's so small that it causes you to bow in total poverty of spirit in order to enter it.

How narrow is the way that leads to life? It is the narrow way of righteousness, a righteousness that actually exceeds that of the scribes and the Pharisees.

Is it any wonder that those who find it are few?

As we begin our study of these verses, I want us to look first at Luke 13:22–30. As you read the passage, mark in distinctive ways the word *saved* and any reference to the *kingdom of God*.

➤ LUKE 13:22–30

And He was passing through from one city and village to another, teaching, and proceeding on His way to Jerusalem. And someone said to Him, "Lord, are there *just* a few who are being saved?" And He said to them, "Strive to enter by the narrow door; for many, I tell you, will seek to enter and will not be able. Once the head of the house gets up and shuts the door, and you begin to stand outside and knock on the door, saying, 'Lord, open up to us!' then He will answer and say to you, 'I do not know where you are from.' Then you will begin to say, 'We ate and drank in Your presence, and You taught in our streets'; and He will say, 'I tell you, I do not know where you are from; DEPART FROM ME, ALL YOU EVILDOERS.' There will be weeping and gnashing of teeth there when you see Abraham and Isaac and Jacob and all the prophets in the kingdom of God, but yourselves being cast out. And they will come from east and west, and from north and south, and will recline *at the table* in the kingdom of God. And behold, *some* are last who will be first and *some* are first who will be last."

1. Write out the question which prompts Jesus' reply.

2. In essence what does Jesus tell them? How does He answer? List His main points below.

3. When is it too late to enter in?

4. What will happen to those who fail to enter in?

Here again, Jesus warns people to strive to enter by the narrow door: "For many, I tell you, will seek to enter and will not be able." Why won't they be able to enter? Because they will try to enter on their own terms. They will think that having eaten and drunk in His presence — having listened to Him teach in their streets — will be enough to get them to heaven. There are people who will knock on the door, saying, "Lord, open to us!" They will call Him "Lord" when He has never been their Lord! And how do we know that? Because Jesus calls them evildoers (Luke 13:27). Oh what weeping and gnashing of teeth there will be on that day when they are not permitted to enter into the kingdom of God because they did not come in by the narrow, small gate.

How narrow is the way? It's as narrow as the following scriptures say it is. As you look up each verse in your Bible, note exactly what it says about the way to the Father or the way to receive His gift of eternal life.

1. John 3:36

2. John 10:9

3. John 14:6

4. Acts 4:12

5. 1 Timothy 2:5

6. 1 John 5:12

Have you taken the narrow way, Beloved? If so, when you share the gospel with others, are you leading them the right way?

DAY FOUR

I don't know about you, Beloved, but I know that the study on the Sermon on the Mount has deepened my concern for the multitudes who sit in church, call themselves Christians, say, "Lord, Lord," and yet do not do the will of the Father.

Are these men and women deluded? Have they been lulled into a sense of false security? No wonder Jesus warns His hearers, "Beware of the false prophets, who come to you in sheep's clothing, but inwardly are ravenous wolves" (Matthew 7:15).

Surely those who call him "Lord, Lord" and yet walk the broad way that leads to destruction have been led astray by false prophets. As the Lord Jesus said, these are teachers who have proclaimed themselves sheep but are actually wolves in disguise. They are the blind leading the blind, and both will fall into the pit of eternal destruction.

Here are men and women who claim to belong to both King and Kingdom, who claim to speak for God and proclaim God's message, and yet their mouths are filled with lies! Is it any wonder Jesus cries out "beware"? Read the following passage with great care. As you read, mark every reference to the false prophets, along with personal pronouns referring to them, such as *their*. Also mark every occurrence of the word *fruit(s)*.

➤ MATTHEW 7:13-27

13 "Enter by the narrow gate; for the gate is wide, and the way is broad that leads to destruction, and many are those who enter by it.

14 For the gate is small, and the way is narrow that leads to life, and few are those who find it.

15 Beware of the false prophets, who come to you in sheep's clothing, but inwardly are ravenous wolves.

16 You will know them by their fruits. Grapes are not gathered from thorn *bushes,* nor figs from thistles, are they?

17 Even so, every good tree bears good fruit; but the bad tree bears bad fruit.

18 A good tree cannot produce bad fruit, nor can a bad tree produce good fruit.

19 Every tree that does not bear good fruit is cut down and thrown into the fire.

20 So then, you will know them by their fruits.

21 Not everyone who says to Me, 'Lord, Lord,' will enter the kingdom of heaven; but he who does the will of My Father, who is in heaven.

22 Many will say to Me on that day, 'Lord, Lord, did we not prophesy in Your name, and in Your name cast out demons, and in Your name perform many miracles?'

23 And then I will declare to them, 'I never knew you; DEPART FROM ME, YOU WHO PRACTICE LAWLESSNESS.'

24 Therefore everyone who hears these words of Mine, and acts upon them, may be compared to a wise man, who built his house upon the rock.

25 And the rain descended, and the floods came, and the winds blew, and burst against that house; and *yet* it did not fall; for it had been founded upon the rock.

26 And everyone who hears these words of Mine, and does not act upon them, will be like a foolish man, who built his house upon the sand.

27 And the rain descended, and the floods came, and the winds blew, and burst against that house; and it fell, and great was its fall."

The verb *beware* is a present, active, imperative verb. When Jesus used the present tense, He was telling us we must continually beware of false prophets. We can never let down our guard. We must constantly be vigilant lest we be led astray. The mood of the verb is imperative, which signifies a command. And because it is in the active voice, the subject (which is implied) is responsible to carry out the action of the verb. You and I are the subject. Our responsibility is to see that we are not led astray!

"But how," you may ask, "can I know a false prophet from a true one? What will keep me from being led astray?" Jesus does not leave you in doubt. He tells you how you can spot a false prophet.

In the passage you just read, you will notice that the verb *bears* appears twice in verse 17. Next to each one of these verbs, write **Pr** for present tense. Do the same for the word *produce* in verse 18, where it is used twice. Then in verse 19 mark the word *bear* with a **Pr**. (Remember that the present tense indicates continuous or habitual action.)

When you finish, you may want to mark your Bible in the same way — or the Sermon on the Mount we have printed in the back of this book.

Now then, according to this passage...

1. How can you identify a false prophet?

2. What significance does the present tense have in verses 17–19?

3. Do you think that a false prophet would call Jesus "Lord"?

4. According to verse 21, who is going to enter the kingdom of heaven?

5. When it says that you will know them by their fruits, what fruits does it mean? Do you think that fruits and doing the will of the Father have any connection? Why or why not?

A false prophet will be recognizable because the fruit of his life will not be in accordance with the will of the Father. He may be a hearer of God's Word and may know God's Word, but his lifestyle will not conform to the will of God. For this reason, his preaching will not call men and women to that narrow, small gate. As a result, he may gather a large crowd of followers — those who want nothing to do with narrow roads or small gates!

In the scripture references that follow, take time to notice the *lifestyle* of false prophets. Look up the following passages in your Bible. Then, from your reading, list in the spaces provided what you learn about false prophets that would help you recognize them.

1. 2 Timothy 3:5–8

2. 2 Peter 2:1–3, 10–19

It is obvious from these passages that false prophets are controlled by the appetites of their flesh, and therefore their focus is on earthly things. You will notice that their preaching appeals to the sensual and to fleshly desires (2 Peter 2:18). Their attitudes reveal almost a flippancy toward spiritual things. You can clearly see their arrogance in that "they do not tremble when they revile angelic majesties, whereas angels who are greater in might and power do not bring a reviling judgment against them before the Lord" (2 Peter 2:10–11).

Their very words are arrogant. They hold to a form of godliness but deny its power (2 Timothy 3:5). When the chips are down, they are lovers of pleasure rather than lovers of God (2 Timothy 3:4). And what do they speak? What is their message?

Look up the following scriptures, and then we will discuss what you have seen. As you look up each one, note what you learn about the *message* of these false prophets.

1. Jeremiah 6:14–15

2. Jeremiah 8:8–12

3. Jeremiah 23:21–40

4. Ezekiel 22:28

5. Acts 20:29–30

6. 2 Timothy 4:3–4

If you have read carefully, Beloved, you have seen that false prophets do not like to "disturb" people. They come with smooth words, saying, "Peace, peace, all is well." They heal the brokenness of people superficially. Their preaching usually does not deal with the issues of sin or with the righteousness that conforms to the lifestyle of Jesus Christ. The cross and denial of self are seldom heard from their pulpits because their desire is to tickle the ears of those who listen.

Yes, their preaching may contain elements of truth…but not the whole counsel of God. The Word of God does not have a prominent place in their preaching unless, of course, it is used out of context. They will lean more toward dreams and visions and prophecies in their presentations, rather than a clear exposition of God's Word.

For the most part, their preaching does not cause men and women to see their poverty of spirit or to mourn over their sins. It does not call people to meekness in the face of disappointment, trials, or suffering. The persecution of the believer because of godliness will not be exalted as a sign of blessing because, as Paul told us, "they are enemies of the cross of Christ" (Philippians 3:18). How can they call their listeners to a cross that they themselves will not bear? How can they proclaim a life of denial when their god is their appetite?

1. Do they care for the sheep? Read Ezekiel 34:1–6, 14–16, 21–24; then list how the false prophets treat their sheep.

2. Now compare what you saw in Ezekiel 34 with 1 Peter 5:1–4. Write down your insights.

Can you understand the seriousness of Jesus' warning about these wolves who masquerade as sheep?

Remember…wolves eat sheep.

DAY FIVE

I will never forget the time I told someone very dear to me that I knew I was going to heaven when I die.

He looked at me and said, "I'm not as conceited as you are. I will wait and see what God decides when He weighs the good against the bad."

Was I conceited?

Can a person *know for certain* he or she possesses the kingdom of heaven? (Notice I said "possesses," not "will possess.")

As we approach the close of our study of the Sermon on the Mount, I feel I must take this final opportunity, beloved and diligent student, to ask you the most important question in this book. Do you know without a shadow of a doubt that you are going to heaven…and how do you know?

Why don't you take a minute and write down how you personally would answer that question, should someone ask you.

I've been finishing up this manuscript over the Christmas holidays. At the same time Jack and I have traveled to Atlanta and to Indianapolis where I have taught at two large events, one for high school students and another for college students. It's been an awesome experience, and I've loved every moment of it (in spite of the conflicting deadlines). I don't know how many we saw come to faith in Jesus Christ, but from what others say, it had to be 150 or more. And most of them were eager, hungry young men who *devoured* the straight teaching of God's Word. What a privilege it was to reason with the college students — fifteen hundred of them — for four and a half hours from the Word of God!

As I've spoken with a variety of individuals in the course of my holiday shopping, travels, and ministry, it's been interesting to note people's varied responses when I ask them about their relationship with Jesus Christ. I'm sure you've received many of the same responses....

"I know I am a Christian or going to heaven because...

> I'm a good person and I've lived by the Golden Rule."
> I've been baptized."
> I am a member of the church."
> I walked the aisle and gave my life to Jesus."
> I've been a Christian ever since I was born."
> God is a God of love, and He wouldn't send anyone to hell."
> I've invited Jesus Christ into my life, I've believed on Him; therefore, I'm saved."
> I've prayed a prayer and asked Christ to come and live inside of me, and I believe He did."

Now, let's suppose you answered in one of the above ways. Basically all those answers are connected to the past — either something you believed or something you did.

So, let me ask another question. What *present evidence* in your life shows you and others that you really are a child of God? Think about it and then write down your answer to this question.

As Jesus brought His sermon to a conclusion, challenging the response of His listeners to His message, so Paul closes his second letter to the Corinthians with a similar admonition:

Test yourselves *to see* if you are in the faith; examine yourselves! Or do you not recognize this about yourselves, that Jesus Christ is in you — unless indeed you fail the test? (13:5)

Think about it: If we could point to a past experience as the only evidence of our salvation, why would it be necessary to test ourselves to see if we really are in the faith?

The verb *test* is in the present tense, indicating a continuous examination of the reality of whether or not Christ is in us. Does that surprise you a little?

According to my study of the Scriptures, I believe in the eternal security of every true believer. I do not believe it is possible for anyone who truly belongs to the Lord Jesus Christ to lose his salvation. You may agree with that position or disagree, but don't miss my next point. Although I believe in the eternal security of the believer and that "the Lord knows those who are His" (2 Timothy 2:19), I must also state this: The only way the believer really knows that he belongs to Jesus Christ and possesses the kingdom of heaven is by the testimony of his changed life, his present and continuous life of overall obedience.

This, I believe, is the point Jesus is making in Matthew 7:21–27. According to these verses, only those who are continually doing the will of the Father will enter the kingdom of heaven. The verb *does* is in the present tense.

The way is so narrow, the issue so critical, Jesus doesn't want His listeners — nor His future readers — to miss it.

Calling Him "Lord" is not enough.

Professing Him as Lord is not enough.

Saying He is our Lord is not enough.

Just because we call Him "Lord" does not mean we are going to go to heaven. Just because we say we are Christians does not mean that we are. Just because we have joined the church and sit in church every Sunday does not mean we possess the kingdom of heaven. As the old saying goes, sitting in a church does not make you a Christian any more than sitting in a garage makes you a car!

Yet, isn't this what many believe? They believe that because they sit in church and go through the motions and the rituals, they are children of God. They believe that because they have been baptized, confirmed, take communion, or "try to live by the Golden Rule," they will go to heaven when they die. They believe that because they "prayed the prayer," they possess eternal life, regardless of the way they live! That's what some of those college students believed!

Yet that is not what Jesus says. He tells us it's not those who say "Lord, Lord" but those who habitually — not perfectly, but habitually, as a lifestyle — do the will of the Father who will enter His kingdom.

Do you realize that the people in Matthew 7 had prophesied in the name of Jesus Christ? They had spoken for God. Not only that, but they had cast out demons and even performed miracles. Their lives bore an element of what you and I would call the supernatural. Yet Jesus tells us that one day He will say to them, "I never knew you; depart from me, you who practice lawlessness" (Matthew 7:23).

Did you also notice that Jesus tells us that although they are saying "Lord," they are practicing lawlessness as a way of life, rather than practicing a life of obedience?

If Jesus is, as Jude 4 says, "our only Master and Lord, Jesus Christ," then although you and I may fail at times, disobey at times, sin at times, we will not practice lawlessness as a habit of life.

The essential character of the believer is obedience. The Sermon on the Mount irrevocably links obedience to faith. They cannot be separated. This is why Jesus brings His teaching to a conclusion in Matthew 7:24 with the words, "Everyone who hears these words of Mine, and acts upon them...."

It is not just hearing but also acting. Those who hear *and act* are like the man who built his house on the rock. No matter what comes, no matter what storms pound on his life, no matter what circumstances rage all around him, his house will not fall because it is founded on the rock. But those who hear Christ's words and do not act upon them are like the man who built his house upon the sand — and great was its fall.

O Beloved, when you examine yourself, is there evidence that Christ is in you? Is your life a life of righteousness? (I'm not saying that you don't sin but that righteousness rather than sin dominates your life.) Do you have a righteousness that surpasses that of the scribes and Pharisees? A righteousness that is internal as well as external? Do you "pursue holiness without which no man will see the Lord"? Is there a hunger and thirst for righteousness within you, and is it being satisfied? Do you recognize that Christ is in you because the Beatitudes are an expression (to one degree or another) of your own personal character? Is your character bringing you into conflict with those who do not know Christ? And what about your conduct? Are you becoming more and more like your heavenly Father?

If you cannot answer these questions in the affirmative, then I invite you to come to that narrow, small gate — the cross — which brings men and women to poverty of spirit and into the kingdom of heaven. Tell God you want Jesus Christ to be your Master and Lord in the fullest sense of the words.

Come.

Confess.

You can't afford not to!

Now let me close our time together with a powerful story taken from *Reaching Toward the Heights* by Richard Wurmbrand.

Russians packed the theater in Moscow. It was the premiere of a new play, "Christ in a Fur." Alexander Rostovtsev, a convinced Marxist who moved among the highest circles of Soviet life, was to play Jesus Christ.

A mockery of an altar occupied center stage. The cross on it was constructed of wine and beer bottles. Full glasses surrounded it. Fat "clergymen" said a drunken "liturgy" consisting of blasphemous formulas. In this sham church, "nuns" played cards, drank, and made ugly jokes while the "religious service" went on.

Then Rostovtsev appeared as Christ, dressed in a robe. He had the New Testament in his hands. He was supposed to read two verses from the Sermon on the Mount, then throw away the book in disgust and shout, "Give me my fur and my hat! I prefer a simple proletarian life."

But something unexpected happened.

The actor did not stop after two verses.

Instead, he continued reading. "Blessed are the gentle, for they shall inherit the earth...." On and on he read through the Sermon while the prompter tried in vain to get him to stop.

Finally he came to the last sentence: "The result was that when Jesus had finished these words, the multitudes were amazed at His teaching."

Rostovtsev then made the sign of the cross in the Orthodox manner and said in a loud but humble way, "Lord, remember me when Thou comest into Thy kingdom."

With that, he left the stage, never to be seen again. The Communists disposed of him.

I imagine that at every rehearsal Alexander Rostovtsev had an opportunity to leaf through the pages of the New Testament. We do not know when God's Word found fertile soil in his heart, but we know that it did. He heard Christ's words and acted upon them. He took the narrow, small gate.

What about you, Beloved?

If you make it your passion to keep on seeking His kingdom and His righteousness, you won't be torn between two masters.

There is only One who is worthy.

THE SERMON ON THE MOUNT

CHAPTER 5

1 And when He saw the multitudes, He went up on the mountain; and after He sat down, His disciples came to Him.

2 And opening His mouth He *began* to teach them, saying,

3 "Blessed are the poor in spirit, for theirs is the kingdom of heaven.

4 "Blessed are those who mourn, for they shall be comforted.

5 "Blessed are the gentle, for they shall inherit the earth.

6 "Blessed are those who hunger and thirst for righteousness, for they shall be satisfied.

7 "Blessed are the merciful, for they shall receive mercy.

8 "Blessed are the pure in heart, for they shall see God.

9 "Blessed are the peacemakers, for they shall be called sons of God.

10 "Blessed are those who have been persecuted for the sake of right-eousness, for theirs is the kingdom of heaven.

11 "Blessed are you when *men* cast insults at you, and persecute you, and say all kinds of evil against you falsely, on account of Me.

12 "Rejoice, and be glad, for your reward in heaven is great, for so they persecuted the prophets who were before you.

13 "You are the salt of the earth; but if the salt has become tasteless, how will it be made salty *again?* It is good for nothing anymore, except to be thrown out and trampled under foot by men.

14 "You are the light of the world. A city set on a hill cannot be hidden.

15 "Nor do *men* light a lamp, and put it under the peck-measure, but on the lampstand; and it gives light to all who are in the house.

16 "Let your light shine before men in such a way that they may see your good works, and glorify your Father who is in heaven.

17 "Do not think that I came to abolish the Law or the Prophets; I did not come to abolish, but to fulfill.

18 "For truly I say to you, until heaven and earth pass away, not the small-est letter or stroke shall pass away from the Law, until all is accomplished.

19 "Whoever then annuls one of the least of these commandments, and

so teaches others, shall be called least in the kingdom of heaven; but whoever keeps and teaches *them*, he shall be called great in the kingdom of
heaven.

20 "For I say to you, that unless your righteousness surpasses *that* of the
scribes and Pharisees, you shall not enter the kingdom of heaven.

21 "You have heard that the ancients were told, 'YOU SHALL NOT COM-
MIT MURDER' and 'Whoever commits murder shall be liable to the court.'

22 "But I say to you that everyone who is angry with his brother shall be
guilty before the court; and whoever shall say to his brother, 'Raca,' shall
be guilty before the supreme court; and whoever shall say, 'You fool,' shall
be guilty *enough to go* into the fiery hell.

23 "If therefore you are presenting your offering at the altar, and there
remember that your brother has something against you,

24 leave your offering there before the altar, and go your way; first be reconciled to your brother, and then come and present your offering.

25 "Make friends quickly with your opponent at law while you are with
him on the way, in order that your opponent may not deliver you to the
judge, and the judge to the officer, and you be thrown into prison.

26 "Truly I say to you, you shall not come out of there, until you have
paid up the last cent.

27 "You have heard that it was said, 'YOU SHALL NOT COMMIT ADUL-
TERY';

28 but I say to you, that everyone who looks on a woman to lust for her
has committed adultery with her already in his heart.

29 "And if your right eye makes you stumble, tear it out, and throw it
from you; for it is better for you that one of the parts of your body perish,
than for your whole body to be thrown into hell.

30 "And if your right hand makes you stumble, cut it off, and throw it
from you; for it is better for you that one of the parts of your body perish,
than for your whole body to go into hell.

31 "And it was said, 'WHOEVER SENDS HIS WIFE AWAY, LET HIM GIVE
HER A CERTIFICATE OF DIVORCE';

32 but I say to you that everyone who divorces his wife, except for *the*

cause of unchastity, makes her commit adultery; and whoever marries a divorced woman commits adultery.

33 "Again, you have heard that the ancients were told, 'YOU SHALL NOT MAKE FALSE VOWS, BUT SHALL FULFILL YOUR VOWS TO THE LORD.'

34 "But I say to you, make no oath at all, either by heaven, for it is the throne of God,

35 or by the earth, for it is the footstool of His feet, or by Jerusalem, for it is THE CITY OF THE GREAT KING.

36 "Nor shall you make an oath by your head, for you cannot make one hair white or black.

37 "But let your statement be, 'Yes, yes' or 'No, no'; and anything beyond these is of evil.

38 "You have heard that it was said, 'AN EYE FOR AN EYE, AND A TOOTH FOR A TOOTH.'

39 "But I say to you, do not resist him who is evil; but whoever slaps you on your right cheek, turn to him the other also.

40 "And if anyone wants to sue you, and take your shirt, let him have your coat also.

41 "And whoever shall force you to go one mile, go with him two.

42 "Give to him who asks of you, and do not turn away from him who wants to borrow from you.

43 "You have heard that it was said, 'YOU SHALL LOVE YOUR NEIGH-BOR, and hate your enemy.'

44 "But I say to you, love your enemies, and pray for those who perse-cute you

45 in order that you may be sons of your Father who is in heaven; for He causes His sun to rise on *the* evil and *the* good, and sends rain on *the* right-eous and *the* unrighteous.

46 "For if you love those who love you, what reward have you? Do not even the tax-gatherers do the same?

47 "And if you greet your brothers only, what do you do more *than others?* Do not even the Gentiles do the same?

48 "Therefore you are to be perfect, as your heavenly Father is perfect.

CHAPTER 6

1 "Beware of practicing your righteousness before men to be noticed by them; otherwise you have no reward with your Father who is in heaven.

2 "When therefore you give alms, do not sound a trumpet before you, as the hypocrites do in the synagogues and in the streets, that they may be honored by men. Truly I say to you, they have their reward in full.

3 "But when you give alms, do not let your left hand know what your right hand is doing

4 that your alms may be in secret; and your Father who sees in secret will repay you.

5 "And when you pray, you are not to be as the hypocrites; for they love to stand and pray in the synagogues and on the street corners, in order to be seen by men. Truly I say to you, they have their reward in full.

6 "But you, when you pray, go into your inner room, and when you have shut your door, pray to your Father who is in secret, and your Father who sees in secret will repay you.

7 "And when you are praying, do not use meaningless repetition, as the Gentiles do, for they suppose that they will be heard for their many words.

8 "Therefore do not be like them; for your Father knows what you need, before you ask Him.

9 "Pray, then, in this way:

'Our Father who art in heaven,

Hallowed be Thy name.

10 'Thy kingdom come.

Thy will be done,

On earth as it is in heaven.

11 'Give us this day our daily bread.

12 'And forgive us our debts, as we also have forgiven our debtors.

13 'And do not lead us into temptation, but deliver us from evil. [For Thine is the kingdom. and the power, and the glory, forever. Amen.]'

14 "For if you forgive men for their transgressions, your heavenly Father will also forgive you.

15 "But if you do not forgive men, then your Father will not forgive your transgressions.

16 "And whenever you fast, do not put on a gloomy face as the hypocrites *do*, for they neglect their appearance in order to be seen fasting by men. Truly I say to you, they have their reward in full.

17 "But you, when you fast, anoint your head, and wash your face

18 so that you may not be seen fasting by men, but by your Father who is in secret; and your Father who sees in secret will repay you.

19 "Do not lay up for yourselves treasures upon earth, where moth and rust destroy, and where thieves break in and steal.

20 "But lay up for yourselves treasures in heaven, where neither moth nor rust destroys, and where thieves do not break in or steal;

21 for where your treasure is, there will your heart be also.

22 "The lamp of the body is the eye; if therefore your eye is clear, your whole body will be full of light.

23 "But if your eye is bad, your whole body will be full of darkness. If therefore the light that is in you is darkness, how great is the darkness!

24 "No one can serve two masters; for either he will hate the one and love the other, or he will hold to one and despise the other. You cannot serve God and mammon.

25 "For this reason I say to you, do not be anxious for your life, *as to* what you shall eat, or what you shall drink; nor for your body, *as to* what you shall put on. Is not life more than food, and the body than clothing?

26 "Look at the birds of the air, that they do not sow, neither do they reap, nor gather into barns, and *yet* your heavenly Father feeds them. Are you not worth much more than they?

27 "And which of you by being anxious can add a *single* cubit to his life's span?

28 "And why are you anxious about clothing? Observe how the lilies of the field grow; they do not toil nor do they spin,

29 yet I say to you that even Solomon in all his glory did not clothe himself like one of these.

30 "But if God so arrays the grass of the field, which is *alive* today and tomorrow is thrown into the furnace, *will He* not much more *do so for* you, O men of little faith?

31 "Do not be anxious then, saying, 'What shall we eat?' or 'What shall we drink?' or 'With what shall we clothe ourselves?'

32 "For all these things the Gentiles eagerly seek; for your heavenly Father knows that you need all these things.

33 "But seek first His kingdom and His righteousness; and all these things shall be added to you.

34 "Therefore do not be anxious for tomorrow; for tomorrow will care for itself. *Each* day has enough trouble of its own.

CHAPTER 7

1 "Do not judge lest you be judged.

2 "For in the way you judge, you will be judged; and by your standard of measure, it will be measured to you.

3 "And why do you look at the speck that is in your brother's eye, but do not notice the log that is in your own eye?

4 "Or how can you say to your brother, 'Let me take the speck out of your eye,' and behold, the log is in your own eye?

5 "You hypocrite, first take the log out of your own eye, and then you will see clearly to take the speck out of your brother's eye.

6 "Do not give what is holy to dogs, and do not throw your pearls before swine, lest they trample them under their feet, and turn and tear you to pieces.

7 "Ask, and it shall be given to you; seek, and you shall find; knock, and it shall be opened to you.

8 "For everyone who asks receives, and he who seeks finds, and to him who knocks it shall be opened.

9 "Or what man is there among you, when his son shall ask him for a loaf, will give him a stone?

10 "Or if he shall ask for a fish, he will not give him a snake, will he?

11 "If you then, being evil, know how to give good gifts to your children, how much more shall your Father who is in heaven give what is good to those who ask Him!

12 "Therefore, however you want people to treat you, so treat them, for this is the Law and the Prophets.

13 "Enter by the narrow gate; for the gate is wide, and the way is broad that leads to destruction, and many are those who enter by it.

14 "For the gate is small, and the way is narrow that leads to life, and few are those who find it.

15 "Beware of the false prophets, who come to you in sheep's clothing, but inwardly are ravenous wolves.

16 "You will know them by their fruits. Grapes are not gathered from thorn *bushes,* nor figs from thistles, are they?

17 "Even so, every good tree bears good fruit; but the bad tree bears bad fruit.

18 "A good tree cannot produce bad fruit, nor can a bad tree produce good fruit.

19 "Every tree that does not bear good fruit is cut down and thrown into the fire.

20 "So then, you will know them by their fruits.

21 "Not everyone who says to Me, 'Lord, Lord,' will enter the kingdom of heaven; but he who does the will of My Father who is in heaven.

22 "Many will say to Me on that day, 'Lord, Lord, did we not prophesy in Your name, and in Your name cast out demons, and in Your name perform many miracles?'

23 "And then I will declare to them, 'I never knew you; DEPART FROM ME, YOU WHO PRACTICE LAWLESSNESS.'

24 "Therefore everyone who hears these words of Mine, and acts upon them, may be compared to a wise man, who built his house upon the rock.

25 "And the rain descended, and the floods came, and the winds blew, and burst against that house; and *yet* it did not fall, for it had been founded upon the rock.

26 "And everyone who hears these words of Mine, and does not act upon them, will be like a foolish man, who built his house upon the sand.

27 "And the rain descended, and the floods came, and the winds blew, and burst against that house; and it fell, and great was its fall."

28 The result was that when Jesus had finished these words, the multitudes were amazed at His teaching;

29 for He was teaching them as *one* having authority, and not as their scribes.

GROUP
DISCUSSION
QUESTIONS

The following questions are to aid you in leading a discussion of the material covered in each chapter. However, merely having the questions will not be enough for a really lively and successful discussion. The better you know your material, the greater freedom you will have in leading the class. Therefore, Beloved, be faithful in your study and remain dependent upon the ministry of the Holy Spirit, who is there to lead you and guide you into all truth and who will enable you to fulfill the good work God has foreordained for you.

As you prepare to lead your class in a discussion of the week's material, I suggest you pray and ask the Father what your particular class needs to learn and how you can best cover the material. Pray with pen in hand. Make a list of what the Lord shows you. Then create your own questions or pick the questions from this list which will help stimulate and guide the class members in the Lord's direction within the time you have. As you do this, remember the class members will find the greatest sense of accomplishment in discussing what they have learned, so try to stick to the subject at hand. In your discussion, make sure that the answers and insights come from the Word of God and are always in accordance with the whole counsel of God. (As the leader, if you have time, it would be ideal to read the entire book first so you understand the scope of the material covered in this study.)

Please know I thank our Father for you and your willingness to assume this critical role of establishing God's people in God's Word as that which produces reverence for Him. Press on, valiant one. He is coming, bringing in the kingdom in all its glory, and His reward is with Him to give to each one of us according to our deeds.

CHAPTER ONE

1. As you read the Sermon on the Mount, what made the most significant impression?

2. What did you learn about the kingdom of heaven?

3. How would you summarize Jesus' teaching in these chapters?

4. Which verse do you think best expresses the message of the Sermon on the Mount?

5. Using the Sermon on the Mount, describe the kind of righteousness that exceeds the righteousness of the scribes and Pharisees.

6. If some shall be called "least" in the kingdom of heaven and some called "great," what determines the difference between them?

7. Do you look forward with anticipation or with fear to the judgment spoken of in 2 Corinthians 5:10 and Romans 14:10? Give the reason for your answer. If you feel dread, what changes will you make in your life?

8. If the foundation upon which we build is Jesus Christ, what might represent gold, silver, and precious stones? What might represent wood, hay, and stubble? What is the quality of your work?

9. What are the four aspects of the "kingdom" and the "kingdom of heaven"?

10. Describe the picture in your mind as you read the description of heaven given in Revelation 4–5. What did you discover about God from these chapters? What insights about the Holy Spirit did you gain?

11. How is the Lord Jesus Christ described in Revelation 4–5?

12. Revelation 21:1–22:5 offers a magnificent description of the new heaven, the new earth, and the new Jerusalem. What did you learn about each of these from this passage?

13. What truth from this lesson made the most impact on your life?

CHAPTER TWO

1. According to Daniel 4, how did Nebuchadnezzar's experience bring him to an understanding of God's sovereignty?

2. How does the knowledge of God's sovereignty impact your thinking about anxiety, fear, and trials?

3. As you read the account of the rich young ruler in Mark 10:17–27, what did you learn about the kingdom of heaven?

4. What instructions did Jesus give the young man? What was the ruler's response? What did reviewing the Ten Commandments reveal about the rich young ruler?

5. In Jesus' parable about the wheat and the tares, what does the wheat represent? What do the tares represent?

6. How can you distinguish between the true wheat and the tares? Who are the reapers, and what will they do with each of these at the end of the age?

7. If the visible kingdom of heaven has not yet arrived, where is the king reigning at the present time?

8. From Matthew 24–25 describe what it will be like when the visible kingdom arrives. On what basis does the king separate the sheep from the goats, and what will be the final outcome for each group?

9. How does Matthew 24–25 parallel the description in the Sermon on the Mount of those who inherit the kingdom of heaven and the earth?

10. Do you believe the Sermon on the Mount is for this age or the age yet to come? Give the reasons for your answer.

11. What impressed you the most about this week's study?

CHAPTER THREE

1. Is the lifestyle depicted by the Sermon on the Mount possible to achieve in today's society? State the reason for your answer.

2. What do Genesis 8:21 and Jeremiah 17:9 teach us about the condition of the human heart apart from Christ?

3. What did you learn from Romans 7:14–24 about the law and man's ability to keep the law?

4. What is the solution to Paul's struggle in Romans 7?

5. According to Jesus, what makes us a slave of sin? How can we be freed from slavery to sin?

6. What did you learn from Romans 6:1–7 about the old self or old man? What happened to the body of sin according to verse 6?

7. To what does Roman 6 liken our baptism? What is the relationship of baptism to the freedom from sin?

8. What does it mean to walk in newness of life? Describe the contrast in Romans 8:1–17 between walking in the Spirit and walking in the flesh.

9. How does the New Covenant differ from the Old Covenant of law? What does the New Covenant do for mankind according to Jeremiah 31:33–34; 32:38–40 and 2 Corinthians 3:2–9?

10. Have you ever feared you might walk away from God? What have you learned about God that addresses that fear?

11. How would you describe a person who is poor in spirit?

12. How can you daily live the lifestyle of the Sermon on the Mount?

CHAPTER FOUR

1. After reading Matthew 5:21–26, what do you think is the true intent of the Law?

2. If the Pharisees followed the letter of the Law and practiced their righteousness before men in order to be noticed by men, how can our righteousness exceed theirs? What must be different about us?

3. What does Jesus teach about burning anger towards a brother, calling him "good for nothing," or calling him a fool? According to this passage, when does murder really begin?

4. What is the difference between the kind of anger that can lead to murder and the righteous anger that abhors sin?

5. According to Matthew 5:28, how serious is entertaining lust in our thoughts?

6. How does God view adultery? Where can adultery lead, according to Galatians 5:19–21? How would you answer someone who said, "Doesn't God understand that sex permeates our culture? Aren't we just covered by grace?"

7. How does God feel about divorce? Has divorce touched your own life directly or indirectly? What are its effects?

8. According to Matthew 5:33, what does the Law say about making false vows? How well do you keep your word to God and to others?

9. Would your friends describe you as a person of honesty and integrity? Where is your integrity weak, and how can you work to change this?

CHAPTER FIVE

1. In reviewing the laws in Exodus 21:1, 12–36, Leviticus 24:17–22, and Deuteronomy 19:10–21, what did you learn about God's view of sin and its punishment? Do you think God is too harsh, and if so, why do you think so?

2. What did you learn as you listed the words *blood, purge,* and *witness?*

3. How does our judicial system compare to God's system? How do you think our country would be affected by implementing God's Law with swiftness and efficiency?

4. Why was the law "an eye for an eye" given? According to Mark 12:28–34 and Romans 13:8–10, what is the true basis for the law?

5. From reading 1 Corinthians 13:1–8, how do you see love fulfilling the Law?

6. As you read Matthew 6, what did you find to be the most piercing statements? In which of the following areas do you struggle the most? Do you care too much about the opinions of men, find it hard to forgive, struggle with serving only one master, or feel anxious about your temporal life?

7. Can you remember a time when you practiced righteous acts but with unrighteous motives? How did you handle it? What would you do differently now?

8. What did you learn in Matthew 6 about almsgiving? From the passages in Deuteronomy, Proverbs, and Psalms, what connection did you see between giving and blessing?

9. Evaluate your motives for giving. Are you allowing the Father who sees in secret to repay you in secret?

10. Have the class end by praying for each other.

CHAPTER SIX

1. How would you describe your prayer life? When do you pray, and what prompts you to pray?

2. What did you learn about your relationship with God by the first index sentence of Jesus' prayer: "Our Father who art in heaven, hallowed be Thy name"? What is the role of worship in communicating with God?

3. What is the focus of the next index sentence: "Thy kingdom come, Thy will be done"? Is God your first allegiance? Are you yielded to His will, and if so, how does your life demonstrate your submission?

4. "Give us this day our daily bread...." Why do you think Jesus places His petition after the first two index sentences? How often does God desire us to come to Him with our needs?

5. Does John 14:13 indicate that God will always give us whatever we ask? Give a reason for your answer.

6. As you seek forgiveness for your debts, is it hard for you to forgive? What is meant by "Forgive us our debts, *as we also* have forgiven others"?

7. What does Jesus mean by "Lead us not into temptation but deliver us from evil"? How would *preventative* prayer benefit your daily life?

8. How does Jesus close His lesson in prayer?

9. Have you ever practiced fasting? What did you learn about fasting from Matthew 6:16–18? What did you learn from Isaiah 58:1–12?

10. According to Isaiah 58:6–7, what is God's chosen fast? As you reviewed the many occasions and the many reasons for fasting, was your spirit stirred inside you? What could you do in response?

11. What prevents you from fasting? What situations in your own life could be impacted by focused prayer and fasting before the Lord?

CHAPTER SEVEN

1. What comes to your mind as you read Matthew 6:19–21? What does it mean to "lay up for yourselves treasures in heaven"?

2. How do you keep from laying up treasures on earth? According to Matthew 6:22–23, where does the seduction by possessions begin? What attracted Eve to the forbidden fruit?

3. What is God's chief rival in our society today? What things consume the most time and energy in your life? What things are you most anxious about?

4. Does relying solely on God's provision relieve us of the responsibility of working? What did you see from 2 Thessalonians 3:6–15 about living an undisciplined life?

5. What behavior did Paul model regarding work in 2 Thessalonians 3:6–15? What was Paul's command in verse 10?

6. How are we to balance our need to depend solely on God's provision yet lead disciplined, productive lives? How does the word *first* relate to this question?

7. Do your priorities fall into line with Matthew 6:33–34? If not, what changes will you make?

8. If you follow God's priorities, what will be God's response in your life?

CHAPTER EIGHT

1. In Matthew 7:1–5 Jesus instructs the people about judging others. In your own words, what is His warning in verse two?

2. What does it mean to "first take the log out of your own eye"? What does Jesus call the one who judges without doing this?

3. What makes the judgment that Jesus discusses in Matthew 7:1–5 wrong?

4. What parallels do you see between Matthew 7:1–5 and Romans 2:1–6, 17–24?

5. If we are not to judge, how can we deal with a brother in sin? What are God's specific instructions in James 5:19–20 and Galatians 6:1?

6. What is to be our attitude when dealing with a brother in sin? From James 5:19–20 and Galatians 6:1, how does the proper attitude of the restorer benefit the one in sin?

7. How can you know if you are judging righteously or out of human motives? Describe the situation Paul writes of in Romans 14. How does Romans 14:15 instruct us to walk?

8. What are God's instructions regarding judging one another's differences? In your own life, how will you "pursue the things which make for peace and the building up of one another"?

9. How do Philippians 3:2–3, 17–19 and 2 Peter 2:1–2 relate to Matthew 7:6?

10. Matthew 7:15–20 warns us to beware of false prophets. Are you able to recognize the "bad fruit"? What might "bad fruit" look like? What insight does 1 John 4:1–6 give to help us discern between the spirit of truth and the spirit of error?

11. Are you grounded solidly in God's Word so that you can recognize bad fruit and false doctrine? Please state the reason for your answer. Have you examined your own heart so that you may judge righteously? Do you need to admit that you have been wrong in judging another?

CHAPTER NINE

1. What is the key to living a life of righteousness that exceeds the righteousness of the scribes and Pharisees? What are the instructions given in Matthew 7:7–12?

2. What point does Jesus make by telling the story in Luke 11:5–13? Do you think He was telling us that even though He's our friend, He is reluctant to give us what we need?

3. Why do you think persistence in prayer is so important?

4. From Matthew 22:34–40, what did you learn about the relationship between love and the Law? How does Romans 13:1–8 expand your understanding of this relationship?

5. What was the question asked of Jesus in Luke 13:22–30? What do you think is the essence of His answer? What will happen to those who fail to enter?

6. How narrow is the way into heaven? What is the only way to enter?

7. In Matthew 7:15 the verb *beware* is in the present tense. What kind of action does the present tense denote?

8. How can we identify a false prophet? What tense of the verb *bear* is used in Matthew 7:17? Why is this important?

9. What is the connection between doing the will of God and the fruit you bear? What is the lifestyle of the false prophets?

10. Do false prophets display humility in their lives? Discuss the reasons for your answer based on the texts in 2 Timothy, 2 Peter, Jeremiah, Ezekiel, and Acts.

11. If someone asked if you are certain of entering heaven when you die, how would you answer? What reasons would you give?

12. What is the most significant lesson you've learned during the last nine weeks?

13. Close by praying for one another.

NOTES

CHAPTER ONE: WHAT IS THE KINGDOM OF HEAVEN?

1. "Finally Home" by Don Wyrtzen

CHAPTER FOUR: TORN BETWEEN TWO MASTERS

1. J. Dwight Pentecost, *The Sermon on the Mount: Contemporary Insights for a Christian Lifestyle* (Portland: Multnomah, 1982), 112.

CHAPTER SIX: PRAYING AND FASTING GOD'S WAY

1. Pentecost, *The Sermon on the Mount,* 127.
2. Reuben A. Torrey, *The Power of Prayer* (Grand Rapids: Zondervan, 1955), 75–77.
3. For an in-depth study of the names of God, see Kay Arthur, *Lord, I Want to Know You* (Sisters, Ore.: Multnomah, 1992).

CHAPTER SEVEN: THE DESIRE FOR THINGS

1. James Montgomery Boice, *The Sermon on the Mount* (Grand Rapids: Zondervan, 1972), 192.
2. Pentecost, *The Sermon on the Mount,* 158.
3. "Christmas Eve in Romania," in *A Bible for Russia,* vol. 1, no. 10, December 1983, 3–4.

CHAPTER NINE: DO YOU POSSESS THE KINGDOM OF HEAVEN?

1. Marie Chapian, *Of Whom the World Was Not Worthy* (Minneapolis: Bethany, 1978), 156–58.

DISCOVER GOD'S TRUTHS
FOR YOURSELF

Every book in Kay Arthur's powerful Lord Bible study series is designed to help you study inductively — to examine God's Word in depth and discern His truths for yourself, rather than relying on interpretations by others.

You can learn more about this life-changing study method in the revolutionary *International Inductive Study Bible,* the only Bible on the market that teaches you how to examine each book of the Bible — chapter by chapter — completely on your own.

Look for the *International Inductive Study Bible* at your local Christian bookstore.

For information about Kay's teaching ministry and about other study materials, write or call:

Precept Ministries
P. O. Box 182218
Chattanooga, Tennessee 37422
Attention: Information Department
(423) 892-6814